SproutCore Web Application Development

Creating fast, powerful, and feature-rich web applications using the SproutCore HTML5 framework

Tyler Keating

PUBLISHING

BIRMINGHAM - MUMBAI

SproutCore Web Application Development

First published: September 2013

Production Reference: 1180913

Published by Packt Publishing Ltd.
Livery Place
35 Livery Street
Birmingham B3 2PB, UK.

ISBN 978-1-84951-770-6

www.packtpub.com

Cover Image by Tyler Keating (tyler@sproutcore.com)

Credits

Author
Tyler Keating

Reviewers
Peter Bergström
Mitch Oliver
Dave Porter
Ido Ran

Acquisition Editor
Pramila Balan

Lead Technical Editor
Anila Vincent

Technical Editors
Manan Badani
Aparna Chand
Vivek Pillai
Adrian Raposo

Project Coordinator
Rahul Dixit

Proofreader
Mario Cecere

Indexer
Priya Subramani

Graphics
Abhinash Sahu

Production Coordinator
Nitesh Thakur

Cover Work
Nitesh Thakur

About the Author

Tyler Keating is the current head of the SproutCore project, and one of the foremost experts on SproutCore, and on writing native caliber web applications using HTML5 and JavaScript.

Although he began his career as an Electrical Engineer at SaskTel, a persistent desire to write software eventually led him to new jobs of writing desktop apps, then server-side web apps, then native mobile apps, and most recently, SproutCore, best of all the world's apps. He currently runs his own consulting company, 7x7 Software Inc, which provides professional software development services, as well as SproutCore training and support.

Whether speaking, or writing, Tyler strives to be a compassionate and conscientious source, who recognizes that nothing is ever black or white, but nevertheless tries to clear the shades of grey, and deliver something concrete and usable to every receiver.

He lives in Regina, Canada, with his wife and three daughters.

About the Reviewers

Peter Bergström is originally from Sweden. He moved to the San Francisco Bay Area when he was a teenager and has been enjoying living there ever since.

Peter got his undergraduate degrees in Computer Science and Economics from UC Santa Cruz and a graduate degree in Computer Engineering from Santa Clara University.

For his graduate thesis, he wrote an experimental application, *PaperCube*, which explored a new way to navigate academic citation networks using web-based visualizations.

After school, he worked at Apple as a user interface engineer at MobileMe (formerly .Mac) leading the development of the Calendar web client. Peter then developed apps for eBay and Apple when he was at Strobe.

Currently, he is the engineering lead for the iOS consumer team at Groupon.

When he is not at a keyboard, he can usually be found biking or running the plentiful hills of the Bay Area.

Mitch Oliver is a Software Developer living with his wife and kids in Cincinnati, OH. He has enjoyed tinkering with computers since he was 9 years old. As time went by, he worked with languages from BASIC to C++ to Ruby, across the OS spectrum. These days, he whiles away his time mining Rubies and brewing Coffeescript for Roadtrippers.com.

Dave Porter is a rich web application developer and SproutCore core team member based in Boston, Massachusetts, where he lives with his lovely wife and an exuberant dog. He began experimenting with SproutCore with Version 1.0, and has been developing with it in earnest since 2010. He has contributed features, bug fixes, and memory improvements and is spearheading the discussion on several upcoming API overhauls. In early 2012, he left the strictures of his Fortune-500 developer job and struck out on his own, freelancing for companies in San Francisco, LA, Vancouver, Toronto, New York, and India. When not working, he enjoys globetrotting, eating adventurously, and writing.

Ido Ran started to play with computers around kindergarten, and did professional work at the age of 15. He works in different and interesting teams, doing work ranging from database-stored-procedures to hiding information inside pictures.

He is always looking for new technologies and new ways to work in teams. That's how he keeps himself sharp and ready for his next challenge.

He is happily married and has 3 dogs, who also like to learn about programming.

www.PacktPub.com

Support files, eBooks, discount offers and more

You might want to visit www.PacktPub.com for support files and downloads related to your book.

Did you know that Packt offers eBook versions of every book published, with PDF and ePub files available? You can upgrade to the eBook version at www.PacktPub.com and as a print book customer, you are entitled to a discount on the eBook copy. Get in touch with us at service@packtpub.com for more details.

At www.PacktPub.com, you can also read a collection of free technical articles, sign up for a range of free newsletters and receive exclusive discounts and offers on Packt books and eBooks.

http://PacktLib.PacktPub.com

Do you need instant solutions to your IT questions? PacktLib is Packt's online digital book library. Here, you can access, read and search across Packt's entire library of books.

Why Subscribe?

- Fully searchable across every book published by Packt
- Copy and paste, print and bookmark content
- On demand and accessible via web browser

Free Access for Packt account holders

If you have an account with Packt at www.PacktPub.com, you can use this to access PacktLib today and view nine entirely free books. Simply use your login credentials for immediate access.

Table of Contents

Preface

The purpose of this book is twofold. The first is to teach you everything you need to know about the application development framework, SproutCore. As the first official SproutCore book, written by the head of the project, this book is the most in-depth and complete introduction to the framework anywhere in existence. In this book we will comprehensively look at every component of SproutCore, including the runtime environment, the powerful model, view and controller layers, the less familiar, but equally important application state, data interface layers, and many other supporting technologies that are built into SproutCore. We also go through hundreds of examples, hints, and tips to get you comfortable and productive with SproutCore as quickly as possible.

The second purpose is to enable you to build and deploy professional quality web applications as quickly as possible. As you will find, SproutCore's features can be described in terms of how that particular feature improved the process of real-world software development and web app deployment. As you read through the book, you will be introduced to the components of SproutCore along with the reasoning behind each and the manner in which you can use each for your real-world projects.

SproutCore is the result of developing several of the most advanced and ambitious web applications that have ever existed and so connecting you with that experience gained is a key purpose of this book.

What this book covers

Chapter 1, *Introducing SproutCore*, introduces the framework, covers how and when to use it, and works through a tutorial of a fully functioning SproutCore application.

Chapter 2, *The Runtime Environment*, covers the core technologies that we will use and build upon in all SproutCore applications.

Chapter 3, The View Layer, covers the structure of the Model-View-Controller (MVC) paradigm in SproutCore along with the view layer specifically.

Chapter 4, The Model Layer, covers the model and data interface layers for synchronizing and managing client-side and server-side data.

Chapter 5, The Controller Layer, covers the Controller and Application State layers for controlling and connecting all the parts together into a cohesive application.

Chapter 6, Testing, Building, and Deploying, completes the entire software development process in order to test, build, and ultimately deploy a real application.

What you need for this book

To follow along with the tutorial in this book, you will need to install the SproutCore framework and build tools. The framework and tools are available for Microsoft Windows, OS X, and Linux and the instructions are included in *Chapter 1, Introducing SproutCore*. Further instructions may be found at `http://sproutcore.com`.

Who this book is for

This book is intended for software developers who are already doing web app development and are looking to tackle more ambitious projects akin to Apple's iCloud web apps or non-web software developers who are looking to move into web application development and still apply their skills and knowledge within a software developer oriented web framework.

Conventions

In this book, you will find a number of styles of text that distinguish between different kinds of information. Here are some examples of these styles, and an explanation of their meaning.

Code words in text are shown as follows: " The first function, `module()`, is used for starting a new group of tests."

A block of code is set as follows:

```
config :my_app, :required => [
  :'sproutcore/desktop',
  :'sproutcore/datastore',
  :'sproutcore/statechart'
]
```

When we wish to draw your attention to a particular part of a code block, the relevant lines or items are set in bold:

```
// Resume the previous match.
resumeMatch: function () {
  this.gotoHistoryState('matchState');
}
}),
```

Any command-line input or output is written as follows:

```
$ mkdir frameworks
$ cd frameworks
$ mkdir my_framework
```

New terms and **important words** are shown in bold. Words that you see on the screen, in menus or dialog boxes for example, appear in the text like this: "Right now, we're only going to focus on tests within the **Apps** section, where we see our **Contacts** app is listed".

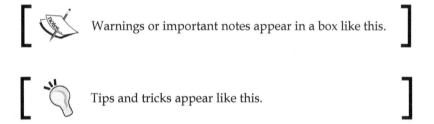

> Warnings or important notes appear in a box like this.

> Tips and tricks appear like this.

Reader feedback

Feedback from our readers is always welcome. Let us know what you think about this book—what you liked or may have disliked. Reader feedback is important for us to develop titles that you really get the most out of.

To send us general feedback, simply send an e-mail to feedback@packtpub.com, and mention the book title via the subject of your message.

If there is a topic that you have expertise in and you are interested in either writing or contributing to a book, see our author guide on www.packtpub.com/authors.

Customer support

Now that you are the proud owner of a Packt book, we have a number of things to help you to get the most from your purchase.

Downloading the example code

You can download the example code files for all Packt books you have purchased from your account at http://www.packtpub.com. If you purchased this book elsewhere, you can visit http://www.packtpub.com/support and register to have the files e-mailed directly to you.

Errata

Although we have taken every care to ensure the accuracy of our content, mistakes do happen. If you find a mistake in one of our books—maybe a mistake in the text or the code—we would be grateful if you would report this to us. By doing so, you can save other readers from frustration and help us improve subsequent versions of this book. If you find any errata, please report them by visiting http://www.packtpub.com/submit-errata, selecting your book, clicking on the **errata submission form** link, and entering the details of your errata. Once your errata are verified, your submission will be accepted and the errata will be uploaded on our website, or added to any list of existing errata, under the Errata section of that title. Any existing errata can be viewed by selecting your title from http://www.packtpub.com/support.

Piracy

Piracy of copyright material on the Internet is an ongoing problem across all media. At Packt, we take the protection of our copyright and licenses very seriously. If you come across any illegal copies of our works, in any form, on the Internet, please provide us with the location address or website name immediately so that we can pursue a remedy.

Please contact us at copyright@packtpub.com with a link to the suspected pirated material.

We appreciate your help in protecting our authors, and our ability to bring you valuable content.

Questions

You can contact us at questions@packtpub.com if you are having a problem with any aspect of the book, and we will do our best to address it.

1
Introducing SproutCore

In this book we will learn everything we need to know about SproutCore, which is one of the most exciting and powerful application development frameworks in existence. As you will discover, SproutCore is a very large topic and covers a lot of ground, so before we even start discussing SproutCore at a high level, let's begin with a brief history.

SproutCore has actually been around for quite a long time in terms of the web, having been created by entrepreneur *Charles Jolley*, back in 2007. Charles created SproutCore to build a mail client, but was soon hired by Apple to grow the framework further and develop several even larger scale applications. Indeed you will likely recognize some of these web applications and may even remember the amazement when people first saw SproutCore apps such as mobileMe delivering a native-like look and feel in the browser without the use of plug-ins.

Until then, the Web 2.0 movement had largely failed to deliver on its promise of replacing the software of the desktop. Of course there are exceptions, but overall, the slew of web 2 apps that appeared were slow and clunky and lacked a lot of the basic features and refinement we had expected in the software. Oddly enough as mobile has gained in popularity, the advancement of web apps has actually slowed down. For instance, compared to the desktop, the network latency for mobile is horrendous and the type of web apps that are delivered a page at a time from a server are almost unusable.

However, and this is why I'm writing this book, this does not need to be the case! With SproutCore apps, the user feedback is instantaneous, lists can be scrolled effortlessly through hundreds of thousands of items. Also, there is drag-and-drop and keyboard control. The apps can run offline and overall the software built with SproutCore feels feature-rich, responsive, and robust. On top of this, SproutCore apps are 100 percent compatible across even less than the modern browsers, all without the use of plug-ins!

Perhaps best of all though, is that SproutCore is, and always will be completely free to use for you and me. As an open source framework, SproutCore gains experience in real world deployments and grows as professionals contribute that experience back into the source for us to use. That is why we're here and that is why whether you're building a new multi-platform social app or replacing an outdated internal management tool, now is the best time to learn about SproutCore.

In this chapter we will cover the following:

- Understanding the SproutCore approach
- Knowing when SproutCore is the right choice
- Building your first SproutCore application:
    - Installing SproutCore
    - Creating a project
    - Adding an app to the project
    - Designing your user interface
    - Modeling your data
    - Connecting it all together
    - Working with user input

Understanding the SproutCore approach

In the strictly technical sense, I would describe SproutCore as an open source web application development framework. As you are likely a technical person interested in web application development, this should be reassuring. And if you are interested in developing web applications, you must also already know how difficult it is to keep track of the vast number of libraries and frameworks to choose from. While it would be nice if we could say that there was one true way, and even nicer if I could say that the one true way was SproutCore; this is not the case and never will be the case. Competing ideas will always exist, especially in this area because the future of software is largely JavaScript and the web.

So where does SproutCore fit ideologically within this large and growing group? To best describe it, I would ask you to picture a spectrum of all the libraries and frameworks one can use to build a web application. Towards one end are the small single-feature libraries that provide useful helper functions for use in dynamic websites.

As we move across, you'll see that the libraries grow and become combined into frameworks of libraries that provide larger functions, some of which start to bridge the gap between what we may call a website and what we may call a web app. Finally, at the other end of the spectrum you'll find the full application development frameworks. These are the frameworks dedicated to writing software for the web and as you may have guessed, this is where you would find SproutCore along with very few others.

First, let me take a moment to argue the position of full application development frameworks such as SproutCore. In my experience, in order to develop web software that truly rivals the native software, you need more than just a collection of parts, and you need a cohesive set of tools with strong fundamentals. I've actually toyed with calling SproutCore something more akin to a platform, rather than a framework, because it is really more than just the framework code, it's also the tools, the ideas, and the experience that come with it.

On the other side of the argument, there is the idea of picking small pieces and cobbling them together to form an application. While this is a seductive idea and makes great demos, this approach quickly runs out of steam when attempting to go beyond a simple project. The problem isn't the technology, it's the realities of software development: customization is the enemy of maintainability and growth. Without a native software like structure to build on, the developers must provide more and more glue code to keep it all together and writing architecturally sound code is extremely hard. Unfortunately, under deadlines this results in difficult to maintain codebases that don't scale. In the end, the ability to execute and the ability to iterate are more important than the ability to start.

Fortunately, almost all of what you need in an application is common to all applications and so there is no need to reinvent the foundations in each project. It just needs to work and work exceptionally well so that we can free up time and resources to focus on attaining the next level in the user experience. This is the SproutCore approach.

SproutCore does not just include all the components you need to create a real application. It also includes thousands of hours of real world tested professional engineering experience on how to develop and deploy genre-changing web applications that are used by millions of people. This experience is baked into the heart of SproutCore and it's completely free to use, which I hope you find as exciting a prospect as I do!

Knowing when SproutCore is the right choice

As you may have noticed, I use the word "software" occasionally and I will continue to do so, because I don't want to make any false pretenses about what it is we are doing. SproutCore is about writing software for the web. If the term software feels too heavy or too involved to describe your project, then SproutCore may not be the best platform for you.

A good measure of whether SproutCore is a good candidate for your project or not, is to describe the goals of your project in normal language. For example, if we were to describe a typical SproutCore application, we would use terms such as:

- "rich user experience"
- "large scale"
- "extremely fast"
- "immediate feedback"
- "huge amounts of data"
- "fluid scrolling through gigantic lists"
- "works on multiple browsers, even IE7"
- "full screen"
- "pixel perfect design"
- "offline capable"
- "localized in multiple languages"
- and perhaps the most telling descriptor of them all, "like a native app"

If these terms match several of the goals for your own project, then we are definitely on the right path.

Let me talk about the other important factor to consider, possibly the most important factor to consider when deciding as a business on which technology to use: developer performance. It does not matter at all what features a framework has if the time it takes or the skill required to build real applications with it becomes unmanageable. I can tell you first hand that custom code written by a star developer quickly becomes useless in the hands of the next person and all software eventually ends up in someone else's hands.

However, SproutCore is built using the same web technology (HTML, JavaScript and CSS) that millions are already familiar with. This provides a simple entry point for a lot of current web developers to start from. But more importantly, SproutCore was built around the software concepts that native desktop and mobile developers have used for years, but that have barely existed in the web. These concepts include:

- Class-like inheritance, encapsulation, and polymorphism
- **Model-View-Controller** (**MVC**) structure
- Statecharts
- Key-value coding, binding, and observing
- Computed properties
- Query-able data stores
- Centralized event handling
- Responder chains
- Run loops

While there is also a full UI library and many conveniences, the application of software development principles onto web technology is what makes SproutCore so great.

When your web app becomes successful and grows exponentially, and I hope it does, then you will be thankful to have SproutCore at its root. As I often heard *Charles Jolley*, the creator of SproutCore, say:

> "*SproutCore is the technology you bet the company on.*"

Building your first SproutCore application

Now that we've gone through some of the theory behind SproutCore, let's jump right in to see it in action. Don't be concerned if some of this first application seems like magic, we'll go into much more detail in the later chapters. For now it's good enough to get SproutCore installed and to gain a feel for SproutCore web app development.

Installing SproutCore

SproutCore is made of two parts: the JavaScript framework and the build tools. The JavaScript framework runs in the browser and powers your application, while the build tools provide a development environment and the ability to build your application so that it may be most efficiently deployed.

 The build tools are written in **Ruby**, but you do *not* need to know Ruby in order to use SproutCore. It is simply the language that the command-line tools were written in and how the framework is distributed. It does mean that you will need to have the Ruby interpreter installed.

Installing Ruby

Although SproutCore's build tools should technically work on Ruby 1.8, the better support, inclusion of **RubyGems** and large performance gain of 1.9 means it's best if you install the latter. If you already have Ruby 1.9 installed, you can skip this section.

Since there are many options for installing Ruby, rather than attempting to provide instructions for every system out there, it is best if you choose the method that best suits your environment from the official Ruby website: `http://www.ruby-lang.org/en/downloads/`.

To verify your Ruby installation, simply run the following from the command line as shown in the following screenshot:

```
$ ruby -v
```

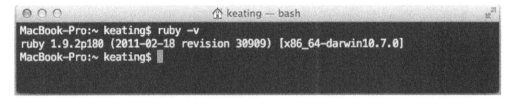

 I prefer using Ruby 1.9.2 rather than 1.9.3, because 1.9.3 has problems including libyaml and has deprecated some of the code used by RubyGems. It doesn't seem to affect anything, but the warnings are annoying.

Once you've got Ruby installed, it's time to get SproutCore.

Installing the SproutCore gem

The SproutCore gem includes the command-line build tools as well as the JavaScript framework. At the time of this writing, the latest version of SproutCore was 1.10. To install it, simply run the following from the command line:

```
$ gem install sproutcore
```

Once it completes, you can verify the installation with the following:

```
$ sproutcore version
```

To learn of more options available to use with the sproutcore command, use:

```
$ sproutcore help
```

```
MacBook-Pro:~ keating$ sproutcore help
Tasks:
  sproutcore build [TARGET..]                                              ...
  sproutcore build-number TARGET                                           ...
  sproutcore docs [TARGET..]                                               ...
  sproutcore gen generator Namespace[.ClassName] [--target=TARGET_NAME] [--f...
  sproutcore help                                                          ...
  sproutcore help [TASK]                                                   ...
  sproutcore init PROJECT [APP]                                            ...
  sproutcore manifest [TARGET..]                                           ...
  sproutcore server                                                        ...
  sproutcore version                                                       ...

Options:
      [--project=PROJECT]
      [--mode=MODE]
      [--logfile=LOGFILE]
  -b, [--build=BUILD]
      [--build-targets=BUILD-TARGETS]  # Targets to build (excluding their depe
ndencies)
      [--dont-minify]                  # Disables minification for the build.
  -v, [--verbose]
  -V, [--very-verbose]
      [--help]

MacBook-Pro:~ keating$
```

Creating a project

Every SproutCore application belongs to a SproutCore project. This allows you to create multiple apps as part of a single project and share resources among them (more on this later). A SproutCore project is simply a directory that contains the related apps, frameworks and themes as well as a Buildfile for the entire project.

To generate an empty project directory that we can use for experimentation, we can use the `sproutcore gen` command.

For a project, we will use the project generator and so we will simply run `sproutcore gen project` from the command line. If you have a directory used for development projects, you may want to `cd` to it first.

Let's create a new project called `sc_experiments`. To create the project, open a terminal window and type the following as shown in the following screenshot:

```
$ sproutcore gen project sc_experiments
```

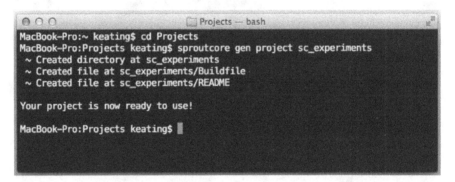

As we can see from the output, the discussed command created a directory called `sc_experiments` as well as two files: `Buildfile` and `README`.

The README file is for your own documentation. Feel free to rename it, remove it or replace it with whatever you like. The Buildfile is important however and must be included. This file is used to instruct the build tools as to how to build the apps within your project. By default it simply requires the complete SproutCore framework for all the apps in the project. This is illustrated in the following screenshot:

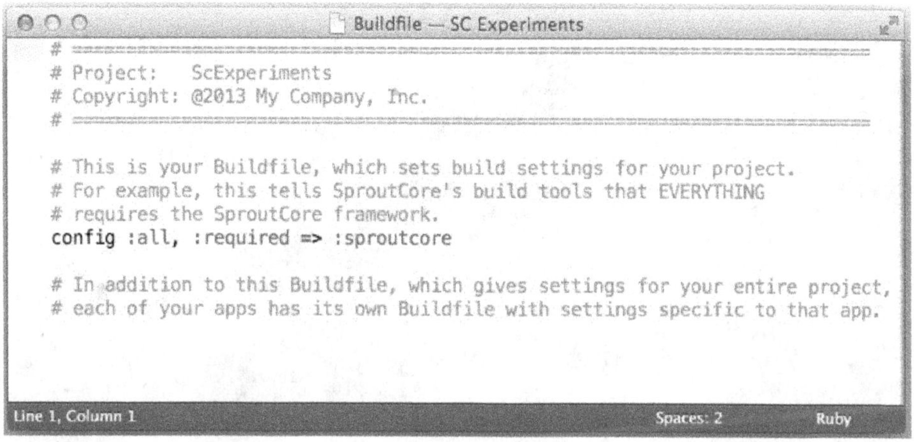

We will look at more sophisticated Buildfile settings in *Chapter 6, Testing, Building and Deploying*, but for now we can leave it as it is.

Adding an app to the project

Now that we have SproutCore installed and a project directory to work with, it's time to create our first app. Let's start with a simple address book app, that we'll call Contacts. Our address book will contain individual contacts and we'll be able to view and group the contacts. You'll also be able to add, remove, and modify the contacts and the groups.

To generate a skeleton for Contacts, we'll turn once more to the sproutcore gen command. Go back to the terminal and run the following as shown:

```
$ cd sc_experiments

$ sproutcore gen app Contacts
```

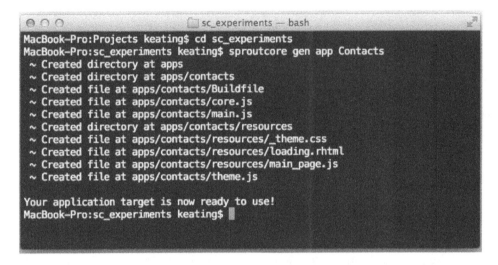

Now let's launch the app and see what we have. To serve the web app locally for debugging purposes, we use the SproutCore development server. To start it, open up another terminal window and type the following:

```
$ sproutcore server
```

Go ahead and open `http://localhost:4020/contacts` in your favorite browser as shown in the following screenshot:

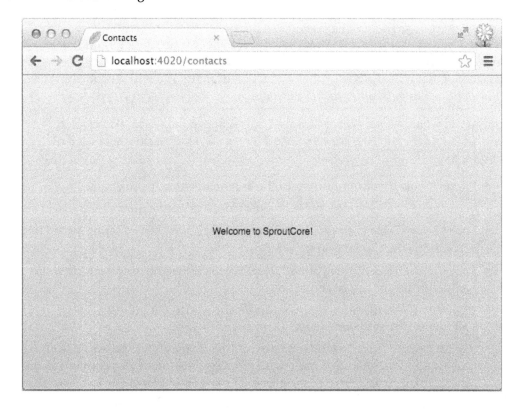

SproutCore apps are just static files, but these static files still need to be served to a browser in order to load correctly. The development server, `sproutcore server` or `sc-server` for short, does a simple build of your project and serves it locally at `http://localhost:4020`. The server also proxies requests to remote servers as indicated by your `Buildfile`. This allows you to avoid the Same Origin Policy rule that would otherwise prevent your locally running app in the `localhost` domain from connecting with APIs on your production domain. We will see more on this in *Chapter 6, Testing, Building and Deploying*.

Now just as when we generated a project, `sproutcore gen app` also created some basic folders and files for us to use. Here is a brief description of each file and directory:

- `apps/`: This directory houses all the apps within your project
- `contacts/`: This directory houses the Contacts application
- `Buildfile`: This is similar to the project's Buildfile, but contains instructions specific to the Contacts app
- `core.js`: This contains your `SC.Application` instance and is the first file loaded from the application code
- `main.js`: This file launches your application once the browser is ready and all JavaScript has been loaded
- `resources/`: This directory contains all the images, style sheets and other assets that you wish to bundle with your application. It also contains page files, which house the preconfigured UI panes and views
- `resources/_theme.css`: This style sheet simply defines the `$theme` variable for use with the CSS styles
- `resources/loading.rhtml`: The contents of this file will be inserted into the built `index.html` file while the the application code loads and is removed when the application launches
- `resources/main_page.css`: This style sheet contains a basic style for the main page defined in `main_page.js`
- `resources/main_page.js`: This file defines an `SC.Page` container that holds all the panes and views that will make up the *main* page of your app
- `resources/theme.js`: This file defines the `SC.Theme` instance for the app. By default it extends the `SC.AceTheme` instance

Designing your user interface

In user-focused development, it's often good to build the interface pieces first and enable them behind the scenes later one component at a time. As a side benefit, this gives us something to get into people's hands early on in order to get valuable feedback.

For our Contacts app, we will follow a tried and true address book layout such as the following:

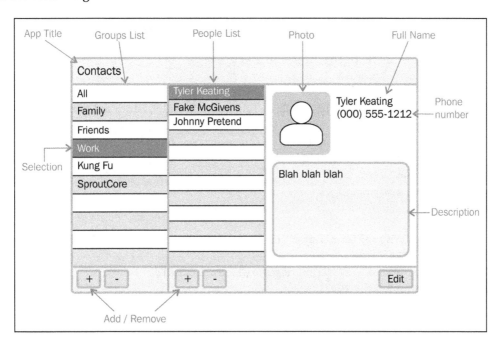

To create an interface with SproutCore we use a declarative approach in JavaScript, which may seem normal if you're coming from native software development, but new if you're accustomed to working directly with HTML. Although SproutCore has toyed with using templates in the past, these attempts have always turned out to perform worse from both an execution performance and a developer performance point of view. For now, I ask you to trust that the style we'll use ends up both faster to write and faster to run.

When starting to lay out a page, the best approach is to start from the outside and work our way in. From the previous figure, it appears that we have four major containing boxes: the toolbar, the groups list, the contacts list, and the contact detail.

Open up main_page.js in a text editor of your choice and replace the content of mainPane with the following:

```
mainPane: SC.MainPane.design({

  childViews: ['toolbarView', 'splitView'],

  // The top header of the page.
  toolbarView: SC.ToolbarView.design({}),

  // Flexible container for the lists and details.
  splitView: SC.SplitView.design({
    // Place this below the toolbarView.
    layout: { top: 32 },

    childViews: ['groupsPanel', 'contactsPanel', 'detailPanel'],

    // The list of groups and group control buttons.
    groupsPanel: SC.View.design(SC.SplitChild, {
      minimumSize: 200,
      size: 250
    }),

    // The list of contacts for the group and contact control
buttons.
    contactsPanel: SC.View.design(SC.SplitChild, {
      minimumSize: 200,
      size: 250
    }),

    // The details for the selected contact.
    detailPanel: SC.View.design(SC.SplitChild, {
      autoResizeStyle: SC.RESIZE_AUTOMATIC,
      minimumSize: 400
    })

  })

})
```

The preceding code gives us our four containing views: toolbarView, groupsPanel, contactsPanel, and detailPanel. You will have noticed that the child views are defined by name in the parent view's childViews array. We also used a couple predefined SproutCore views, SC.ToolbarView and SC.SplitView. The SC.ToolbarView just adds some nice default styling while the SC.SplitView will allow the user to resize the width of each panel. In order to make the split view work properly, we mix the SC.SplitChild mixin to each of these child views and define a few settings for how each child should behave. A mixin is a collection of properties and methods that can be added to an object or class. Mixins and the use of design, extend, and create will be covered in detail in *Chapter 2, The Runtime Environment*.

Let's add all the remaining components of our page. First we'll add the title to the toolbar and give it the value of "Contacts".

```
// The top header of the page.
toolbarView: SC.ToolbarView.design({
  childViews: ['titleView'],

  titleView: SC.LabelView.design({
    controlSize: SC.LARGE_CONTROL_SIZE,
    layout: { centerY: 0, height: 24, left: 10, width: 200 },
    value: "Contacts"
  })
}),
```

Notice that we declare the layout of the titleView at the same time. By default all instances of SC.View (which includes SC.ToolbarView and SC.LabelView in this case) will be positioned absolutely according to the layout property. Absolute positioning allows the browser to avoid any reflow when the DOM is updated and is therefore much faster to use. It's actually a very flexible approach when used with single page apps.

You'll also notice that we use the controlSize property. Several SproutCore controls, such as SC.LabelView, use the controlSize property to affect the style applied. In this case, we use SC.LARGE_CONTROL_SIZE to give us a label style that will fit a height of 24 pixels. We can override this in CSS later if we wish.

Next we'll add both of the lists with their respective control bars as shown in the following code:

```
// The list of groups and group control buttons.
groupsPanel: SC.View.design(SC.SplitChild, {
  minimumSize: 100,
  size: 250,

  childViews: ['list', 'controlBar'],

  list: SC.ScrollView.design({
    layout: { bottom: 44 },
    contentView: SC.ListView.design({
      content: ["A", "B", "C", "D", "E", "F"]
    })
  }),

  controlBar: SC.ToolbarView.design({
    anchorLocation: SC.ANCHOR_BOTTOM
  })
}),

// The list of contacts for the group and contact control buttons.
contactsPanel: SC.View.design(SC.SplitChild, {
  minimumSize: 100,
  size: 250,

  childViews: ['list', 'controlBar'],

  list: SC.ScrollView.design({
    layout: { bottom: 44 },
    contentView: SC.ListView.design({
      content: ["1", "2", "3", "4", "5", "6", "7", "8", "9", "10"]
    })
  }),

  controlBar: SC.ToolbarView.design({
    anchorLocation: SC.ANCHOR_BOTTOM
  })
}),
```

Since we know that we want our lists to scroll, we've placed each SC.ListView within an SC.ScrollView. We also gave our lists some placeholder content to use while we're still designing the page.

Let's add the buttons to the next view. Insert the following into both the `controlBar` views as shown in the following code:

```
controlBar: SC.ToolbarView.design({
  anchorLocation: SC.ANCHOR_BOTTOM,

  childViews: ['addButton', 'removeButton'],

  addButton: SC.ButtonView.design({
    controlSize: SC.HUGE_CONTROL_SIZE,
    layout: { centerY: 0, left: 10, width: 40, height: 30 },
    title: '+'
  }),

  removeButton: SC.ButtonView.design({
    controlSize: SC.HUGE_CONTROL_SIZE,
    layout: { centerY: 0, left: 60, width: 40, height: 30 },
    title: '-'
  })
})
```

Here we're going to use `SC.ButtonView` to get nice buttons. This is probably a good time to mention that all of the pre-built SproutCore views and controls along with code snippets for each can be previewed on the SproutCore Showcase page (`http://showcase.sproutcore.com`). When you're done with this tutorial, you may want to browse and see what other views you may want to use.

Finally, we just need to create the detail panel. Considering the many options for presenting all the data that can be attached to a contact, this could become very complicated. For now, we'll keep it simple and use an image, first name, last name, telephone number, and description.

Go ahead and add the following to `detailPanel` as shown in the following code:

```
detailPanel: SC.View.design(SC.SplitChild, {
  autoResizeStyle: SC.RESIZE_AUTOMATIC,
  minimumSize: 350,

  childViews: ['image', 'fullName', 'telNumber', 'description',
'controlBar'],

  image: SC.ImageView.design({
    layout: { left: 20, top: 20, height: 120, width: 120 },
    scale: SC.BEST_FIT,
    value: sc_static('sproutcore-128.png')
  }),
```

```
      fullName: SC.LabelView.design({
        layout: { left: 160, top: 50, height: 25, width: 150 },
        value: "Tyler Keating"
      }),

      telNumber: SC.LabelView.design({
        layout: { left: 160, top: 75, height: 25, width: 100 },
        value: "(000) 555-1212"
      }),

      description: SC.TextFieldView.design({
        isEditable: false,
        isTextArea: true,
        layout: { left: 20, top: 160, bottom: 52, right: 20 },
        value: "Author of the amazing Beginner's Guide to SproutCore
book and just generally an all around nice human being."
      }),

      controlBar: SC.ToolbarView.design({
        anchorLocation: SC.ANCHOR_BOTTOM,

        childViews: ['editButton'],

        editButton: SC.ButtonView.design({
          layout: { centerY: 0, right: 10, width: 80, height: 24 },
          title: 'Edit'
        })

      })
    })
  })
```

We should point out the two new views we introduced here: SC.ImageView and SC.TextFieldView. As you can guess, SC.ImageView displays an image and in this case we are using a SproutCore build tools command, sc_static() to get the path to an image included in the framework as our placeholder value.

By the way, you might not know it yet, but we also solved the problem of fitting a source image into the aspect ratio of the frame we want to use, by setting the scale property. In this case we're using best fit scaling, which ensures the source image fits within the frame without stretching. Again, the SproutCore Showcase page has examples of the different image options.

The other new control we used is SC.TextFieldView, which we set to behave as a text area (isTextArea: true) and which we set to be non-editable (isEditable: false).

And that completes our basic user interface. Why don't you reload http://localhost:4020/contacts in your browser and have a look at what we've got. I think you'll agree that in very little time, we have made a decent looking prototype for our Contacts app as illustrated in the following screenshot:

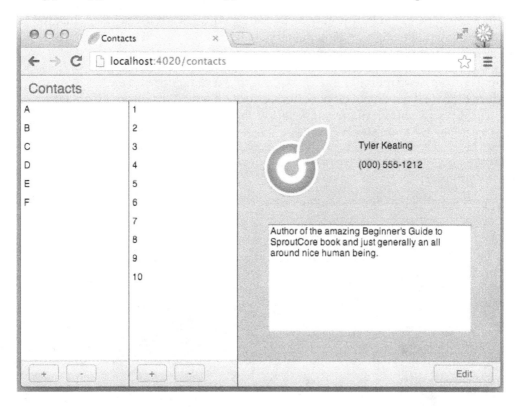

Modeling your data

SproutCore contains an extremely powerful Model layer made up of records, data stores, and data sources. When you use the command line generator to create a new project, the default `core.js` file contains a fixtures-backed data store, which is a powerful development tool.

Now it's often the case that the server API is being defined at the same time as the application is being built or it may be the case that we want to use fixed data for development and testing. In either event, we'll see how easy it is to define records and provide fixture data in SproutCore for us to work with.

From the brief description of our Contacts app we came up with earlier, we can deduce that we'll need at least two models to start with: Groups and Contacts. Each group will contain many contacts and to keep it simple, we'll allow a contact to belong to only one group.

First, let's generate the records. From within your project run the following two commands:

```
$ sproutcore gen model Contacts.Group
```

```
MacBook-Pro:sc_experiments keating$ sproutcore gen model Contacts.Group
 ~ Created directory at fixtures
 ~ Created file at fixtures/group_fixtures.js
 ~ Created directory at models
 ~ Created file at models/group_model.js
 ~ Created directory at tests
 ~ Created directory at tests/models
 ~ Created file at tests/models/group_test.js

Your model is now ready to use!
MacBook-Pro:sc_experiments keating$
```

```
$ sproutcore gen model Contacts.Contact
```

```
● ● ○                          sc_experiments — bash
MacBook-Pro:sc_experiments keating$ sproutcore gen model Contacts.Contact
  ~ Created file at fixtures/contact_fixtures.js
  ~ Created file at models/contact_model.js
  ~ Created file at tests/models/contact_test.js

Your model is now ready to use!
MacBook-Pro:sc_experiments keating$ ▮
```

As we've come to expect, this generated a few directories and files for us according to the SproutCore convention. On the first run, it added a `models` directory, a `tests` directory with a `models` sub-directory and a `fixtures` directory.

The purpose of each directory should be fairly self-explanatory. Our model classes go in `models`, our unit tests go in `tests` and our fixture data goes in `fixtures`. In fact, you'll notice that the command already generated stub files in each of these places for our two new record classes: `Contacts.Group` and `Contacts.Contact`.

Now, let's open up the `group_model.js` file inside of the `models` directory and define its attributes. We know that our groups need at least one attribute, a name. You define attributes on the record, using `SC.Record.attr`. Add the name attribute to the `Contacts.Group` model as shown:

```
Contacts.Group = SC.Record.extend(
/** @scope Contacts.Group.prototype */ {

  name: SC.Record.attr(String)

});
```

We can similarly add `firstName`, `lastName`, `telNumber`, `imageURI` and `description` attributes to `Contacts.Contact`.

```
Contacts.Contact = SC.Record.extend(
/** @scope Contacts.Contact.prototype */ {

  firstName: SC.Record.attr(String),
```

```
      lastName: SC.Record.attr(String),

      telNumber: SC.Record.attr(String),

      imageURI: SC.Record.attr(String),

      description: SC.Record.attr(String)

   });
```

Finally, we can add the relationship between the two. First in `Contacts.Group`, indicate that each group has a to-many relationship to its contacts with a `contacts` attribute.

```
// ...

// Each group has many contacts.
contacts: SC.Record.toMany('Contacts.Contact', {
  inverse: 'group'
})

// ...
```

Then add the to-one relationship in `Contacts.Contact` back to the group.

```
// ...

// Each contact has one group.
group: SC.Record.toOne('Contacts.Group', {
  inverse: 'contacts'
})

// ...
```

Next we'll add placeholder data in fixtures that we can work with. Fixtures are simply an array of objects (that is hashes) containing the raw attribute value of each record. You can create whatever data you like to use, provided it has the correct attributes. In a real project, you would tend to start with a small amount of fixture and grow and improve it as the project progresses. Here's an example of one group with two contacts:

```
// Groups
Contacts.Group.FIXTURES = [
```

```
    {
      guid: 'family',
      name: 'Family',
      contacts: ['tyler', 'juanjuan']
    }

  ];

  // Contacts
  Contacts.Contact.FIXTURES = [

    {
      guid: 'tyler',
      firstName: 'Tyler',
      lastName: 'Keating',
      telNumber: '0005551212',
      description: 'Me.',
      group: 'family'
    },

    {
      guid: 'juanjuan',
      firstName: 'Juanjuan',
      lastName: 'Zhao',
      telNumber: '0005552323',
      description: 'Lovely!',
      group: 'family'
    }

  ];
```

Creating fixtures is fairly straightforward, except for one thing. Did you notice that we never defined a guid attribute on our record classes? So where did that come from? It turns out that guid is the default primary key attribute for all subclasses of SC.Record. To identify records, each needs a primary key, which normally would have been set by the server. In this case we make up our own primary keys and use them as references in the contacts and group relationships.

To save your time, we've created a large set of fixtures that you can download from <link>. Simply replace the group_fixtures.js and contact_fixtures.js files in your project with those found in the downloaded directory.

Finally, we're ready to peruse our new data. At this point we have a client side data store, `Contacts.store` (defined in `core.js`), and if you've added the fixture data, we also have several records of type `Contacts.Group` and `Contacts.Contact`.

We haven't connected it to anything, so we won't see any changes in the UI, but we can do everything we need from the browser console. Let's try a few tests.

After you reload the app and open up the browser console, please query the local store for all the groups as shown:

```
> groups = Contacts.store.find(Contacts.Group);
```

See how when we pass the record type that we want to find in the store, we are returned `SC.RecordArray` of all the matching records. Now we'll use one of SproutCore's enumerable helper methods to do a quick inspection of the groups as shown:

```
> groups.getEach('name');
```

Does everything look in order? You should see an array of names for all the fixture groups that you provided. If you're not seeing results similar to the following you should look for syntax errors in the console and double-check your code so far.

Next let's test the relationship between groups and contacts. In the browser's console, have a go with the following:

```
> group = groups.objectAt(0);
```

```
> contacts = group.get('contacts');
```

```
> contacts.getEach('firstName');
```

Again, this is a good time to check that our fixture data matches what we believe we had written. Because we usually create most of the fixture data manually, it's easy to make typing mistakes.

 SproutCore methods almost always return the caller, allowing you to chain them together. For example, the previous three calls could just as easily have been:

```
> groups.objectAt(0).get('contacts').getEach('firstName')
```

Finally, lets take a peak at one of our records, using `toString()`:

```
> contacts.objectAt(0).toString();
```

 Don't worry yet about the use of `objectAt`, `get`, and `getEach`. These are important patterns essential to SproutCore's key value binding and observing, but for now it's enough just to get used to seeing and using them.

Connecting it all together

At this point we have a functioning View layer and a functioning Model layer, but no logic tying it all together into a functioning application. This is where the Controller layer comes into play.

Although you can create advanced application state logic with SproutCore, for our app we are only concerned right now with mapping our Model layer data to our View layer views.

We'll start at the highest point in the data hierarchy, which is the collection of groups.

To manage the group records, we will want to use SC.ArrayController, so turning once more to sproutcore gen, use the following command to generate a groupsController singleton of type SC.ArrayController:

```
$ sproutcore gen controller Contacts.groupsController

SC.ArrayController
```

 The gen controller command creates singleton objects of type SC.ObjectController by default. Passing a class name as the last argument allows us to have it use SC.ArrayController in this case.

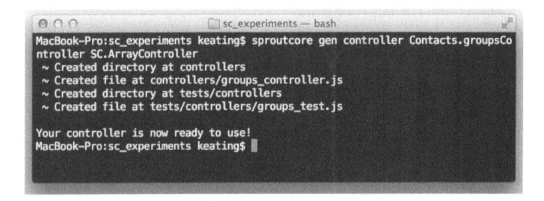

As usual, these statements generated a couple new directories for us according to the SproutCore conventions (./controllers/ and ./tests/controllers/) as well as a couple skeleton files.

Fortunately, since we have mentioned in the command what class of controller we wanted to create, this file doesn't actually need to be changed at all.

Next, we will need a controller for a single selected group, a controller for the contacts of the selected group, and a controller for a single selected contact. In this manner we will have controllers to represent our full data hierarchy.

These commands will create the other controller instances we need:

```
$ sproutcore gen controller Contacts.groupController
$ sproutcore gen controller Contacts.contactsController
SC.ArrayController
$ sproutcore gen controller Contacts.contactController
```

It's a good idea at this point to inspect each file and make sure that you've got the names all correct. I'm sure I'm not the first person that mistyped "contactController" or "contactsController".

As was mentioned earlier, the top of our data hierarchy will be managed by groupsController and therefore this is the controller whose content we will actually set directly. To do this we will set the content to the results of a query on our client side data store. If you haven't guessed it yet, the query will be the same one we first tried out in the browser's console.

Open up main.js inside your app and simply uncomment the example labeled "Step 2". It just so happens that the main.js template contains exactly the code we need. In case the main.js template changes in the future, here is what your main.js should look like for reference:

```
Contacts.main = function main() {

  // Step 1: Instantiate Your Views
  // The default code here will make the mainPane for your
application visible
  // on screen.  If you app gets any level of complexity, you will
probably
  // create multiple pages and panes.
  Contacts.getPath('mainPage.mainPane').append() ;

  // Step 2. Set the content property on your primary controller.
  // This will make your app come alive!
  var content = Contacts.store.find(Contacts.Group);
  Contacts.groupsController.set('content', content);

};
```

Now we'll use SproutCore's incredible binding support to chain our controllers together. Bindings allow changes from one object to propagate to its bound counterparts in an extremely efficient manner. We will use bindings to ensure that our other controller's contents are always in sync.

First, we want our `groupController` to represent the selected group in the `groupsController`. One of the primary functions of an array controller is to manage the selection of its items. To ensure that our `groupController`'s content is the currently selected group in `groupsController`, we will simply bind `groupController`'s content property to `groupsController`'s selection property.

From within `group_controller.js` add the following binding:

```
Contacts.groupController = SC.ObjectController.create(
/** @scope Contacts.groupController.prototype */ {

  contentBinding: 'Contacts.groupsController.selection'

});
```

While we're at it, you may as well update `contacts_controller.js`. Its content should be the contacts array of the current group in `groupController` as shown in the following code:

```
Contacts.contactsController = SC.ArrayController.create(
/** @scope Contacts.contactsController.prototype */ {

  contentBinding: 'Contacts.groupController.contacts'

});
```

And `contact_controller.js` can be updated just like `groupController` was:

```
Contacts.contactController = SC.ObjectController.create(
/** @scope Contacts.contactController.prototype */ {

  contentBinding: 'Contacts.contactsController.selection'

});
```

There is one more step that we should do before we stop and review and that is to also connect our controllers to our view. Similar to how we connected our controllers to each other, we can bind our views to their relevant controllers and everything will just work.

Let's start with our two lists: one of groups and one of contacts for the selected group. Fortunately we have two controllers that fit the bill exactly and so now you should return to main_page.js and update your two list views as shown:

```
// … inside of groupsPanel
list: SC.ScrollView.design({
  layout: { bottom: 32 },

  contentView: SC.ListView.design({
    // The content for this list is contained in
Contacts.groupsController.
    contentBinding: 'Contacts.groupsController.arrangedObjects',

    // If the list selection changes, update the selection on the
controller.
    selectionBinding: 'Contacts.groupsController.selection'
  })
}),
// …

// … inside of contactsPanel
list: SC.ScrollView.design({
  layout: { bottom: 32 },

  contentView: SC.ListView.design({
    // The content for this list is contained in
Contacts.contactsController.
    contentBinding: 'Contacts.contactsController.arrangedObjects',

    // If the list selection changes, update the selection on the
controller.
    selectionBinding: 'Contacts.contactsController.selection'
  })
}),
```

Alright, this seems like a great time to head back to the browser and have a look. What you should see is that our first list is now populated with strange looking references to `Contacts.Group`. These are actually the result of calling `toString()` on each group record and although it may not look like it yet, this is exactly what we want. If you select one of the items from the groups list, you'll see the contacts list update with a similar list of references to `Contacts.Contact`.

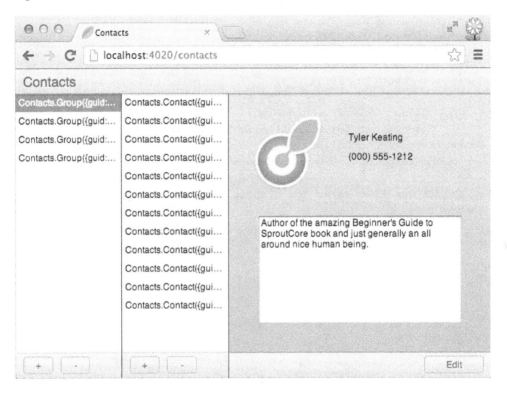

The reason that the list items aren't properly formatted is because we haven't specified what property of our record should be used as the list item's display value. `SC.ListItemView`, the default view used by `SC.ListView`, will use the property named in `contentValueKey` as its value to display.

Since our group records have a `name` property already, we'll simply use that in our list of groups as shown in the following code:

```
// … inside of groupsPanel
contentView: SC.ListView.design({
  // Display the name of each group in the list.
```

```
contentValueKey: 'name',

    // The content for this list is contained in
Contacts.groupsController.
    contentBinding: 'Contacts.groupsController.arrangedObjects',

    // If the list selection changes, update the selection on the
controller.
    selectionBinding: 'Contacts.groupsController.selection'
})
```

But as often is the case, we don't have a direct property to use for display from our other record. For contacts, we really want to use a full name, but the record has two properties: firstName and lastName that make up the full name. It turns out that SproutCore already has an elegant solution to this type of problem, called computed properties.

We can add a new property fullName and make it computed from firstName and lastName. Inside of contact_model.js, add the following property as shown in the following code:

```
fullName: function () {
  var firstName = this.get('firstName'),
  lastName = this.get('lastName');

  return [firstName, lastName].compact().join(' ');
}.property()
```

Now we can set the proper contentValueKey for our other list to be the fullName property of our content as shown in the following code:

```
// … inside of contactsPanel
contentView: SC.ListView.design({
  // Display the full name of each contact in the list.
  contentValueKey: 'fullName',

  // The content for this list is contained in Contacts.
contactsController.
  contentBinding: 'Contacts.contactsController.arrangedObjects',

  // If the list selection changes, update the selection on the
controller.
  selectionBinding: 'Contacts.contactsController.selection'
})
```

Presto! We now have nice looking lists and all that's left is to bind up our detail panel views to the contact controller.

Simply replace the placeholder values in the views with value bindings to `Contacts.contactController` instead as shown in the following code:

```
// … inside of detailPanel
image: SC.ImageView.design({
   layout: { left: 20, top: 20, height: 120, width: 120 },
   scale: SC.BEST_FIT,
   valueBinding: 'Contacts.contactController.imageURI'
}),

fullName: SC.LabelView.design({
   layout: { left: 160, top: 50, height: 25, width: 150 },
   valueBinding: 'Contacts.contactController.fullName'
}),

telNumber: SC.LabelView.design({
   layout: { left: 160, top: 75, height: 25, width: 100 },
   valueBinding: 'Contacts.contactController.telNumber'
}),

description: SC.TextFieldView.design({
   isEditable: false,
   isTextArea: true,
   layout: { left: 20, top: 160, bottom: 52, right: 20 },
   valueBinding: 'Contacts.contactController.description'
}),
```

And with that, we've connected all of our data to our view. All that's left now is to allow the user to modify the data, which brings us to our last task.

Working with user input

Our application is looking really good, but there's no way yet for the user to modify the data. We'll rectify this situation now.

Starting at the top of our data tree again, we want to add the ability to add a new group. Let's enable the + button in the groups column. Open up `main_page.js` and add the following:

```
addButton: SC.ButtonView.design({
   action: 'addGroup',
```

```
      layout: { centerY: 0, left: 10, width: 40, height: 24 },
      target: Contacts,
      title: '+'
   }),
```

This indicates that the action, `addGroup` should be run on the target, `Contacts` (that is our application instance).

> Later we'll use `SC.Statechart` to better organize our application logic, but for now since Contacts is our highest level of application "state", I think it's a good place to put the `addGroup` function.

To implement `addGroup`, add the following to `core.js`:

```
// …
addGroup: function (sender) {
  var dataHash,
    tempGuid;

  // Define data for a new group.
  dataHash = {
    name: 'New Group',
    contacts: []
  };

  // Give our record a temporary unique guid.  If we committed the
record back to the
  // server, the server would generate its own primary key which
would replace this.
  tempGuid = SC.guidFor(dataHash);

  // Simply create the record in the store and our
groupsController content will update
  // automatically.
  Contacts.store.createRecord(Contacts.Group, dataHash, tempGuid);
},
// …
```

That's all there is to it. Each time the groups add button is clicked a new Contacts. Group will be created in the store. Go ahead and try it in the browser if you like. Notice that we don't have to modify the groups list or groups controller code at all to have our user interface update automatically. Isn't that spectacular?

We can implement the addcontact action in a similar manner. Starting in main_page.js, add the action and target to the button as shown in the following code:

```
addButton: SC.ButtonView.design({
  action: 'addContact',
  layout: { centerY: 0, left: 10, width: 40, height: 24 },
  target: Contacts.groupController,
  title: '+'
}),
```

With groups, the application instance was one level higher than the array of groups. For contacts, groupController is one level higher than the array of contacts and is a suitable place for the addContact action.

Then we implement the action in group_controller.js:

```
// …
addContact: function (sender) {
  var contacts,
    content = this.get('content'),
    group,
    dataHash,
    newContact,
    tempGuid;

  // Content is a 'selection'. Only add a contact if that
selection is a single group.
  if (content && content.get('length') === 1) {
    // There is only one group selected, get it.
    group = content.get('firstObject');

    // Define data for a new contact.
    dataHash = {
      firstName: 'New',
      lastName: 'Person',
      group: group.get('id')
    };

    // Give our record a unique guid.  If we committed the record
back to the
    // server, the server would generate its own primary key which
we would
    // replace this with.
```

```
    tempGuid = SC.guidFor(dataHash);

    // Simply create the record in the store and our
groupsController content will
    // update automatically.
    newContact = Contacts.store.createRecord(Contacts.Contact,
dataHash, tempGuid);

    // Add the newContact to the group's contacts array.
    contacts = group.get('contacts');
    contacts.pushObject(newContact);
  }
}
```

Adding a contact is a bit more complex, because we can only add a contact if a single group is selected and we need to update the group's list of contacts at the same time. Once you've tried that out, let's implement our remove actions.

Add actions and targets to the buttons in main_page.js as shown in the following code:

```
// … inside of groupsPanel
removeButton: SC.ButtonView.design({
  action: 'removeGroup',
  layout: { centerY: 0, left: 60, width: 40, height: 24 },
  target: Contacts.groupsController,
  title: '-'
})
// … inside of contactsPanel
removeButton: SC.ButtonView.design({
  action: 'removeContact',
  layout: { centerY: 0, left: 60, width: 40, height: 24 },
  target: Contacts.contactsController,
  title: '-'
})
```

Notice that we're using different controllers for the targets of these actions. This will make more sense once we've implemented the action methods.

First in groups_controller.js:

```
// …
removeGroup: function (sender) {
  var selection = this.get('selection');
```

```
  // Iterate through the selected groups.
  selection.forEach(function (group) {
    // Destroy each group.
    group.destroy();
  });
}
```

and in `contacts_controller.js`:

```
// …
removeContact: function (sender) {
  var content = this.get('content'),
    selection = this.get('selection');

  // Iterate through the selected contacts.
  selection.forEach(function (contact) {
    // Remove the contact from the group's contacts (i.e. our
content).
    content.removeObject(contact);

    // Destroy each contact.
    contact.destroy();
  });
}
```

Hopefully the target of these actions makes more sense now. We chose these controllers because the scope of "removing" depends on the selection that these controllers manage.

Lastly, we want the user to be able to edit the records. `SC.ListView` allows us to edit its displayed property values directly, so we can use it to edit the group names. Simply add `canEditContent: true` to the groups list definition. For example:

```
// … inside of groupsPanel
contentView: SC.ListView.design({
  // Allow the group name to be modified within the list.
  canEditContent: true,
})
  // …
```

Editing a full contact is a bit more difficult. There are multiple fields to edit and we want to support committing and canceling the edit as well as uploading images. For now, I hope that you've seen enough of what you can achieve so quickly in SproutCore and that your appetite has been wetted to delve deeper as we look at SproutCore in greater detail in the later chapters.

Summary

Excellent work, you've made it through a lot of new concepts and even building your first SproutCore app! You should now know what SproutCore is, why it exists and why you would use it; and most importantly you should have successfully installed the platform and seen some of the powerful features in action.

While it all may be a bit overwhelming, don't fear since we will review everything in greater detail soon. For now, this is a good time to reflect on how much functionality we achieved with so little code. If you perused your Contacts application's files once more, I think you'd agree that there is remarkably little code, yet the app in the browser is already exhibiting some advanced behaviors. With only a few more additions we would have something that we could even give to a user. This reminds us that the true power of SproutCore is that it allows us to offload all the time consuming dirty work onto the framework so that we can spend our energy on fine tuning the user experience that will set our application apart.

In the next chapter, we will begin our detailed look into the SproutCore puzzle, starting with the runtime environment. This set of technologies is what really runs our apps at the base level and which provides the foundation for every additional component that SproutCore provides.

2
The Runtime Environment

Much of SproutCore is built on top of a few core technologies that comprise the "runtime environment". You can think of the runtime environment as the foundation that you will build your application on top of. The success story for SproutCore is that its foundation is so well designed, which makes it possible to build extremely large and complex applications while still achieving exceptional performance. Therefore, being able to understand the fundamentals of the runtime environment and how to use it properly is the key to any well-written SproutCore application and in this chapter we will attempt to do just that.

In this chapter we will cover the following:

- Building on SproutCore's object model
- Using mixins to share functionality
- Working with properties and computed properties
- Observing properties for instant updates
- Binding properties for error-free consistency
- Working with enumerables:
    - SC.Array
    - SC.Set
    - Observing enumerables
    - Observing properties on enumerable items
- Understanding the run loop

Building on SproutCore's object model

As you are likely aware, JavaScript uses prototypes and there are no classes in the "class-based object-oriented programming" sense within JavaScript. But in SproutCore, we often refer to classes and objects (that is instances of a class) and the reason for this jargon is in part due to the familiarity of those terms to most developers and in part due to the manner in which we use SproutCore's root class, SC.Object, to organize and enhance our code. Please don't get hung up on the semantics of a prototype versus a class, it really doesn't matter for our purposes.

What you *should* pay attention to though, is that SC.Object is the base of every class within SproutCore and provides the class-like features, such as inheritance, instantiation, mixin support, key-value coding, binding and observing, computed properties, and other conveniences that we will use.

It's probably easier to explain these features through example, so let's first create a subclass of SC.Object. For instance if we had an app, which we'll simply call MyApp, that contained different types of vehicles, we may wish to define a reusable class containing properties shared by all of the vehicles. To do so we simply subclass SC.Object using the extend method. For example:

```
MyApp.Vehicle = SC.Object.extend();
```

To define common properties for the MyApp.Vehicle class, we pass a JavaScript object to the extend method. Here's a nice professional example defining the MyApp.Vehicle class along with its default properties:

```
/** @class
  A vehicle.
*/
MyApp.Vehicle = SC.Object.extend({

  /**
    The make of the vehicle.

    @type String
    @default 'unknown'
  */
  make: 'unknown',

  /**
    The model of the vehicle.

    @type String
    @default 'unknown'
```

```
*/
model: 'unknown',

/**
  The type of the vehicle.

  @type String
  @default null
*/
type: null

});
```

 The property types of the object passed to extend are not restricted to the JavaScript primitives; you can also set functions in order to define instance methods for the new class.

Once the `MyApp.Vehicle` class is defined, we can further subclass it as we like. For example:

```
MyApp.Car = MyApp.Vehicle.extend({

  /**
    The top speed of the car in miles per hour.

    @type Number
    @default 0
  */
  topSpeed: 0,

  /** MyApp.Vehicle override */
  type: 'car',

  /**
    Helper method to convert the given speed in miles per hour to
  kilometers per hour.

    @param {Number} speedMph The speed in mph.
    @returns {Number} The speed in kph.
  */
  calculateSpeedKph: function (speedMph) {
    return speedMph * 1.609344;
  }

});
```

Once we've defined the classes we need for our application, we are able to create the instances of these classes for use. To create a new instance of SC.Object or any of its subclasses, we use the create method. For example, we could create an SC.Object instance as shown:

```
var myObject = SC.Object.create();
```

We would create instances of SC.Object subclasses in the same way as shown:

```
var aVehicle = MyApp.Vehicle.create();
var aCar = MyApp.Car.create();
var aView = SC.View.create();
```

As you would expect, instances inherit the properties of their parent classes and are unique from one another. For example:

```
aVehicle.get('type');   // returns null
aCar.get('type');        // returns 'car'
aVehicle.calculateSpeedKph;   // returns undefined
aCar.speedKph(60);   // returns 96.56064
```

And just like with extend, we can initialize and further configure our object on creation by passing in one or more JavaScript objects. For example:

```
var myObject = SC.Object.create({
  a: 'foo',
  b: 'bar'
});
myObject.get('a'); // returns 'foo'

var fastCar = MyApp.Car.create({ topSpeed: 195 });
fastCar.get('topSpeed');   // returns 195
```

Did you notice in the previous example that we created an instance, myObject, based directly off of SC.Object? While we could have made a subclass and used it to create an instance, it was simpler just to pass the custom properties and methods to the create method. Doing this is a useful way to create singleton objects that can exist for the lifetime of the running application, which is more efficient then defining a subclass and only ever instantiating one object from it.

Before we look at more features of SC.Object, there are two important methods defined within SC.Object that are used when dealing with the object's lifecycle. These two methods are init and destroy. As you might expect, the purpose of the methods is to set up and teardown an object. Therefore if you would like to perform extra initialization on your object as it is created, you would override the init method and likewise, to perform additional cleanup on destruction, you would override the destroy method.

For example:

```
GolfApp.Game = SC.Object.create({

  /** Array of scores for each hole in order. */
  scores: null,

  /** @private */
  init: function () {
    // Always call the superclass method!
    sc_super();

    // Any extra initialization can go here.  For example,
    // Initialize the scores.
    this.scores = [];
  },

  /** @private */
  destroy: function () {
    // Always call the superclass method!
    sc_super();

    // Any extra cleanup can go here.
  }

});
```

There are two important things to recognize about the previous example. The first is that you need to be careful when defining non-primitive values for properties (that is Arrays and JavaScript objects). Notice that the value of the scores property is defined initially as null and later set to the array object in init? If we had rather defined the property as an array, like scores: [], ... , every instance of GolfApp.Game would share the same array object in memory. While the bad players might enjoy sharing their scores with the good players, it's not what we want to happen. Instead, when each instance is created we use init to give that instance a unique scores array.

The second important thing to recognize is that we are able to override the SC.Object class's original init and destroy methods and still call them using sc_super. This is a special class-like behavior added by SproutCore that is not normally easy to accomplish in JavaScript, but with SC.Object it's trivial.

> The `sc_super()` function is not actually a JavaScript function, but a preprocessor command for the build tools. This is one of the few places where the build tools will modify your code and replace `sc_super()` with `arguments.callee.base.apply(this, arguments)`, which looks up the current function on the super class and calls it using the arguments given.

Now that we've learned how to build a simple class hierarchy using `SC.Object`, let's look at further approaches to defining properties that makes it easier to prevent code duplication and keep our hierarchy lightweight.

Using mixins to share functionality

In the previous section we defined subclasses of `SC.Object` that inherit functionality from their parent classes. However, inheritance is too rigid for sharing code among classes that may not directly inherit from a shared parent.

For instance, in a previous example we defined a `MyApp.Vehicle` class and a `MyApp.Car` subclass of it. The `MyApp.Car` subclass added a `topSpeed` property supposedly unique to cars, but of course, `topSpeed` is not unique to cars. What if we had `MyApp.Truck`, `MyApp.Boat`, `MyApp.Plane`, `MyApp.Helicopter`, and other vehicle types? Some of these types will share common traits, such as top speed, but not all traits will be common to all vehicles, such as maximum altitude. How then would we subclass them to reduce redundancy?

While we could try to create hierarchies such as `MyApp.Vehicle | MyApp.GroundVehicle | MyApp.Car | MyApp.Racing`, this would likely end up being both too complex to manage and still not flexible enough for all cases. What about racing trucks, boats, and planes?

Obviously, inheritance is a nice tool for dividing classes into broad channels, but shouldn't be used too granularly. Instead, this type of situation calls for using a mixin that can be applied across multiple classes regardless of their hierarchy. Mixins are very easy to use in SproutCore; they are just regular JavaScript objects. Let's look at how to define and use them.

For example, to create a Raceable mixin containing the traits common to all racing vehicles, we simply define a Raceable JavaScript object:

```
MyApp.Raceable = {

  /**  The total number of races.   */
  numRaces: 0,

  /** The results of each race.   */
  results: null

  /** @private Further initialize the object using this mixin when
it is created. */
  initMixin: function () {
    // Initialize the results hash so that the JS object is unique
to each instance.
    this.results = {};
  },

  /** @private Further clean up the object using this mixin when
it is destroyed. */
  destroyMixin: function () {
    // Any special clean up required?  Not likely, but this
function can do it.
  }

};
```

As you can see, there are two special functions that mixins can provide: `initMixin` and `destroyMixin`. These functions will be run when the object using the mixin is created or destroyed respectively.

You do not call `sc_super()` in `initMixin` or `destroyMixin`.

To apply a mixin to your classes or instances, simply add it as an argument when calling `extend` or `create`. This is illustrated in the following code:

```
// Include the Raceable mixin in all instances of a class.
MyApp.Car = MyApp.Vehicle.extend(MyApp.Raceable);
MyApp.Plane = MyApp.Vehicle.extend(MyApp.Raceable);

// Include the Raceable mixin in certain instances only.
var racingCar = MyApp.Car.create(MyApp.Raceable);
```

Since you can pass multiple arguments to `create` and `extend`, you can include several mixins along with your own custom hashes. For example:

```
// Create a dog instance that has properties of a show pet and a
pedigreed pet.
var myDog = PetsApp.Dog(
    { color: 'black', breed: 'Boston Terrier' },
    PetsApp.Showable,        // Mixin
    PetsApp.Pedigreeable  // Mixin
);
```

> You may wonder about multiple definitions of `initMixin` and `destroyMixin` overriding one another. This is not the case because both of these methods are what are called concatenated properties. Concatenated properties aren't overridden in subclasses, but appended to an array so that each may be applied.

The last thing to know about mixins is that SproutCore includes several prebuilt mixins that you can use to quickly add functionality to your classes. Some that may be of interest to you and that you should research on your own are `SC.Freezable`, `SC.Copyable`, and `SC.Comparable`. For now, it's enough that you are able to recognize the role of a mixin and know how to create and use them.

Working with properties and computed properties

While the class-like features of `SC.Object` are wonderful for creating and managing complex software hierarchies, they are not likely the primary reason you would use `SC.Object` over a regular JavaScript object. Instead, I think you'll find that the most powerful component of `SC.Object` is the key-value coding and the observing features it provides. Or if you don't find that to be the case just yet, you will soon see it in action. In fact, if you followed through the tutorial in *Chapter 1, Introducing SproutCore*, you've already seen how bindings, a technology backed by key-value coding and observing, can magically update your application.

While we will get to bindings soon, we first need to backtrack a bit. Before we bind and observe properties, we need to understand how to always use them properly. For instance, to ensure that changes to our properties will update the observers of those properties, we follow the concept of key-value coding or KVC. If you're familiar with frameworks like Cocoa, you'll already understand this concept, but even if you haven't encountered it yet, it's extremely easy to implement by following one simple rule: always use `get()` to retrieve a property's value and always use `set()` to set it.

For example, if our class has a public property, `lastName`, rather than setting its value directly as shown:,

```
personObj.lastName = 'Keating';
```

We always use the `set` method, as shown:

```
personObj.set('lastName', 'Keating');
```

Doing it the latter way ensures that any observer code for the `lastName` property of `personObj` will execute when the value has changed. If we had instead set it using the dot notation approach, we would have to do all the work manually propagating that change across our app by ourselves, which is not a desirable task.

So while this simple example explains an important reason to always use `set`, it doesn't explain why we need to always use `get` to access the same property. The reason we do use `get` is this, our properties are not always regular properties, they may also be computed properties.

Computed properties are really just special functions that return a value based on some other property or properties. They allow you to expose a single public property in your object's API without requiring the user to understand the internals of how it is calculated; a concept called encapsulation.

We create computed properties by defining a function that we call `property()`. You've already seen a computed property in *Chapter 1, Introducing SproutCore,* the `fullName` property of `ContactsApp.Person`. Let's look at it again:

```
ContactsApp.Person = SC.Object.extend({

  firstName: '',

  lastName: '',

  /** This property is computed from firstName and lastName. */
  fullName: function () {
    var firstName = this.get('firstName'),
    lastName = this.get('lastName');

    return [firstName, lastName].compact().join(' ');
  }.property()

});

// Some example code to use the above.
```

```
var me = ContactsApp.Person.create({ firstName: 'Tyler', lastName:
'Keating' });
me.get('fullName');            // Returns "Tyler Keating"

// Change a dependent property of fullName using KVC
me.set('firstName', 'Trevor');
me.get('fullName');            // Returns "Trevor Keating"

// Don't use '.' notation!
me.fullName;                   // Returns "function () { var

firstName …
```

As you can see, we can access the fullName property at any time and it will always reflects the state of the firstName and lastName properties, as long as we use get and set.

Because get and set are used so frequently within SproutCore they are as efficient as possible, but there is a way that we can make our computed properties even faster. Look at the following example from my browser console, which is based on the code discussed:

```
●○○              Developer Tools – http://localhost:4020/contacts

Elements  Resources  Network  Sources  Timeline  Profiles  Audits  Console

> Person = SC.Object.extend({

    firstName: '',
    lastName: '',

    fullName: function () {
      console.log('Calculating fullName...');
      var firstName = this.get('firstName'),
        lastName = this.get('lastName');

      return [firstName, lastName].compact().join(' ');
    }.property()

  });

  me = Person.create({ firstName: 'Tyler', lastName: 'Keating' });
  ▶ ret {__sc_super__: SC.mixin.K, _kvo_cloned: null, firstName: "Tyler", lastName: "
    Keating", _observers: Array[0]…}
> me.get('fullName');
  Calculating fullName...
< "Tyler Keating"
> me.get('fullName');
  Calculating fullName...
< "Tyler Keating"
>

□  ⟫≡  Q  ⊘  <top frame> ▼  All | Errors  Warnings  Logs  Debug        ⚙
```

Notice that each time we get `fullName` the console message is repeated. However, the value of our computed property hasn't changed and so there is really no need to re-compute it each time. To prevent `fullName` from being re-calculated, we should use the `cacheable()` function.

Let's append the `cacheable()` function to our computed property and observe the output again as shown in the following screenshot:

As you can see from the preceding screenshot, the first time that we get `fullName`, it is calculated, but all successive `get` instances return the cached value. While this is now much more efficient, in particular if our computed property involved complex computations, it does pose a problem. What happens when `firstName` or `lastName` change? As you may have guessed, the value of `fullName` will not yet update accordingly. This is because we have not indicated which properties that `fullName` is dependent on, which we will remedy right now. Since `fullName` is dependent on `firstName` and `lastName`, we simply pass the names of those properties to the `property()` function. This is illustrated in the following screenshot:

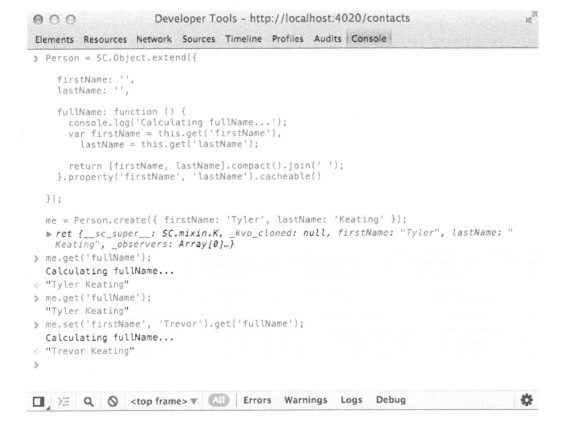

```
Developer Tools - http://localhost:4020/contacts

Elements  Resources  Network  Sources  Timeline  Profiles  Audits  Console

> Person = SC.Object.extend({

    firstName: '',
    lastName: '',

    fullName: function () {
      console.log('Calculating fullName...');
      var firstName = this.get('firstName'),
        lastName = this.get('lastName');

      return [firstName, lastName].compact().join(' ');
    }.property('firstName', 'lastName').cacheable()

  });

  me = Person.create({ firstName: 'Tyler', lastName: 'Keating' });
  ▶ ret {__sc_super__: SC.mixin.K, _kvo_cloned: null, firstName: "Tyler", lastName: "
    Keating", _observers: Array[0]…}
> me.get('fullName');
  Calculating fullName...
⇐ "Tyler Keating"
> me.get('fullName');
  "Tyler Keating"
> me.set('firstName', 'Trevor').get('fullName');
  Calculating fullName...
⇐ "Trevor Keating"
>

☐  ⟩☰  Q  ⊘  <top frame> ▼  ⒶⓁ  |  Errors  Warnings  Logs  Debug                    ⚙
```

> Remember, only getting the computed property runs the property code. Therefore, do not use computed properties to call other functions, this is the role of observers, which we will look at soon. Computed properties should only be used to compute a value.

Can you see how the property doesn't re-calculate until we modify a dependent property? Excellent! we now have an efficient computed property that we can use to simplify our code.

However, so far the computed property we've been using is read-only. This is typically all we need, but it is possible to make computed properties writeable. The way it works is that each time a computed property is accessed via `get` or `set`, the function is passed two arguments: `key` and `value`. In the case of `get`, only the `key` argument will be defined and `value` will be undefined. Knowing this allows us to determine whether the property is being retrieved or set.

Here's an example of our same computed property, now with write support:

```
fullName: function (key, value) {
   if (value !== undefined) { // use !== instead of != to avoid
type coercion
     // Setting fullName.
     var names = value.split(' ');
     this.set('firstName', names[0]);
     this.set('lastName', names[1]);
   }

   var firstName = this.get('firstName'),
   lastName = this.get('lastName');

   return [firstName, lastName].compact().join(' ');
}.property('firstName', 'lastName').cacheable()
```

That concludes our look at accessing properties according to the key-value coding principle. There are a few other convenience methods in `SC.Object` that you will encounter for use with the properties, notably `toggleProperty`, `incrementProperty`, and `decrementProperty`. We won't look at these right now, but the names should explain well enough what they do and all you need to know is that internally they are simply conveniences on top of `get` and `set`.

Let's continue on and observe our properties for changes.

Observing properties for instant updates

While writing an application, you occasionally want to do some action "X" whenever some change "Y" occurs. Traditionally, you may have created a helper function that you would call each time you performed a change. For example, this might result in code that looks something like the following:

```
MyApp.Item = SC.Object.extend({

  quantity: 0,

  updateServer: function () {
    // Sends the new information to the server.
  }

});

// Elsewhere in the code …
var item = MyApp.Item.create();
item.set('quantity', 100);

// Elsewhere in the code at a later date ...
item.updateServer();  // Oops.. missed this.  Don't forget to
update the server!

// Elsewhere in the code …
item.decrementProperty('quantity');

// Elsewhere in the code at a later date ...
item.updateServer();   // Darn it!  DON'T forget to update the

server!!
```

As you can tell by the colorful comments, the approach in the previous example has led to problems in the developer's code over time. Each time the quantity changed, he or she had to remember to call the update helper function. But as the application grew or as people churned in and out of the project, "keep it in the developer's mind" did not work well. Instead, we should let the code itself remember to do the right thing when certain properties change using SproutCore's observers.

The simplest observer can be set up when our object is created using the `observes()` function. Here's an easy improvement on the previous example, that would have saved the developer a few headaches:

```
MyApp.Item = SC.Object.extend({

  quantity: 0,

  updateServer: function () {
    // Sends the new information to the server.
    console.log("Updated the server.");
  }.observes('quantity')

});

var item = MyApp.Item.create();

// Elsewhere in the code ...
item.set('quantity', 100);
  > "Updated the server."

// Elsewhere in the code ...
item.decrementProperty('quantity');
  > "Updated the server."
```

Now each time the quantity changes, the `updateServer()` function runs without us having to remember to manually trigger it, thus simplifying our code and possibly saving us from serious problems in the future.

The `observes` function works by adding observers when an object is created, but we can also easily add observers manually after the object already exists using `addObserver`. To do this, we call `addObserver` on the object and pass in the name of the property to observe along with the callback function. For example:

```
var item = SC.Object.create({ quantity: 0 });

// Manually add an observer.
item.addObserver('quantity', function() {
  // Sends the new information to the server.
  console.log("Updated the server.");
});
```

Obviously, if every instance such as item needed the same observer, it would be easier to make an Item class and use observes like in the first example. However, addObserver works really well when paired with removeObserver. This is a useful pattern when we need to only temporarily observe a property.

To do this, we use alternate arguments for addObserver and pass in a target and method rather than a callback function. Here's an example that begins observation at a certain point and then turns it off again when it is no longer needed:

```
MyApp.Item = SC.Object.extend({

  quantity: 0,

  quantityDidChange: function () {
    // Sends the new information to the server.
    console.log("Updated the server.");
  }

});

var item = SC.Object.create();

// Start observing quantity now (target: item, method:
item.quantityDidChange)
item.addObserver('quantity', item, item.quantityDidChange);

item.set('quantity', 100);
 > Updated the server.

// Stop observing quantity now.
item.removeObserver('quantity', item, 'quantityDidChange');
```

In this way, we don't need to have observers connected and receiving updates if our application happens to not be in a state that can use the updates.

Just as computed properties should only be used to return values, observers should only be used to call functions when a property changes. Try to avoid using observers to set flags such as isReady. Instead, your flags should be computed properties that compute themselves based on the state of the application.

Lastly, we can also observe properties across objects using "property paths". Property paths are simply strings containing chains of property names connected with periods that point to a property in another object. These paths may be relative or absolute.

For example, the absolute path to the `fullName` property on the `MyApp.userController.content` object would be:

```
'MyApp.userController.content.fullName'
```

The relative path within the `userController` object to the same property would be:

```
'.content.fullName'
```

As you can see, absolute paths start with a global object while relative paths begin with a period. Let's look at an example using the property paths discussed:

```
⊖ ○ ○              Developer Tools – http://localhost:4020/contacts                    ⌐

 Elements  Resources  Network  Sources  Timeline  Profiles  Audits  Console

> MyApp.userController = SC.Object.create({

    content: SC.Object.create({
      fullName: 'Timothy Keating'
    }),

    fullNameDidChange: function () {
      var fullName = MyApp.userController.getPath('content.fullName');
      console.log('  Relative fullNameDidChange: ' + fullName);
    }.observes('.content.fullName')

  });

  var myObj = SC.Object.create({

    fullNameDidChange: function () {
      var fullName = MyApp.userController.getPath('content.fullName');
      console.log('  Absolute fullNameDidChange: ' + fullName);
    }.observes('MyApp.userController.content.fullName')

  });

  MyApp.userController.setPath('content.fullName', 'Heather Keating');
    Relative fullNameDidChange: Heather Keating
    Absolute fullNameDidChange: Heather Keating
◄ ▶ SC.Object {__sc_super__: Object, _kvo_cloned: null, content: SC.Object,
    fullNameDidChange: function, _observers: Array[1]…}
> |

 ☐  ⋝  Q  ⊘  <top frame> ▼  ⁜  |  Errors  Warnings  Logs  Debug              ✿
```

This example is simple enough. When I change the value of `fullName`, both observer functions are called because the property paths resolve to the same property on the `content` object.

Did you notice that I used the helpers `getPath` and `setPath`, rather than chaining together `get` and `set`? If I hadn't used `setPath` for instance, the line would have looked like:

```
MyApp.userController.get('content').set('fullName', 'Heather

Keating');
```

There is one more catch though. Are you able to guess it? Pay attention to what happens when I set `content` in the same example:

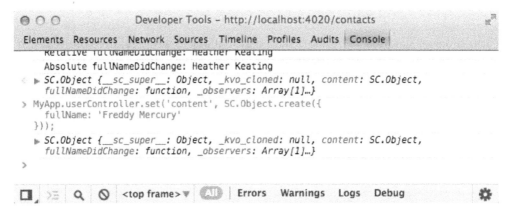

Uh-oh! I swapped out the content and its `fullName` property and neither one of our observers fired. The problem here is that only the last property in the path is observed on the second-to-last object (that is `fullName` is observed on `MyApp.userController.content`). This means that two `fullName` observers are attached to the initial content object and when that initial content object is removed or replaced, our observer code goes with it. The new content object does not automatically get the observers transferred over to it.

To address this, observers (and bindings as we'll see later) recognize a special * property path separator. As I mentioned earlier, the last property named is observed on the second-to-last object named, but with the * separator, all objects named after the star are observed for changes. This means that the following two property paths are essentially the same:

```
'MyApp.userController.content.fullName'
'MyApp.userController.content*fullName'
```

However, by moving the * separator in the path we can observe `fullName` and `content` changes as shown

```
'MyApp.userController*content.fullName'
```

With the property path discussed, `fullName` will be observed on `content` and additionally `content` will be observed on `MyApp.userController`. Let's try it out in an example:

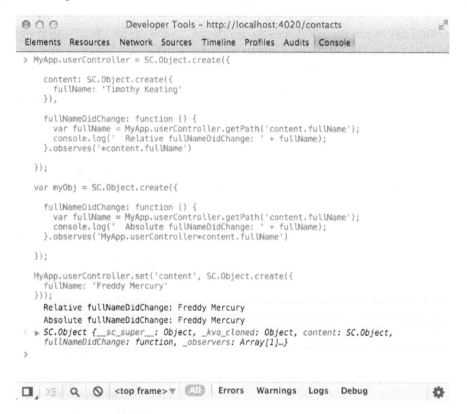

Now when I change either `fullName` of `content` or `content` itself, our observers update accordingly.

 Be aware that each additional chained property in the property path requires more processing to manage. So it's a good idea to only observe what absolutely must be observed.

Binding properties for error-free consistency

At this point, we've already got a great toolkit for working with the properties of our `SC.Object` subclasses, but we don't yet have the proper means to connect separate object properties together. This is where we will turn to SproutCore's bindings. Bindings are another one of those framework features that native software developers have enjoyed for some time, but have not been available in a web framework. I say enjoy for good reason, bindings makes up for clean and magical code. As it turns out, SproutCore's bindings were actually modeled on and so I've heard, improved upon the binding system in Cocoa.

Let's look at why bindings are so important. Here's a screenshot of a SproutCore application of mine called **Hubbub**.

What we're looking at is an item that has been lent out and I've highlighted five areas in red on the screen. These five areas share something in common; they all depend on the isBorrowed property of the selected item. Now if I were to toggle the isBorrowed property from true to false, then the lent count (A) would have to decrement, the button title (B) would have to change, the row style (C) would have to update, the borrower details (D) would have to disappear and the title (E) would need to be modified. Without the means to bind all of these changes to my property I would be left searching out all the relevant parts of the UI and manually updating them. This is why so many web apps have UI consistency problems. As the elements move around, the code to search out and update every property gets more and more complex until it's a nightmare to attempt even the slightest change.

The proper approach, as we've already seen briefly in *Chapter 1*, *Introducing SproutCore*, is to bind our properties together. Binding from one property to another will observe each property for changes and efficiently synchronize the changes between the two.

 What makes bindings so efficient is that they will only synchronize the value once per run loop. If the isBorrowed property from above were toggled 100 times in immediate succession, only the final value would propagate through the app.

Similar to observers, bindings can be created when an object is initialized using a special property naming convention, which is the name of the property followed by the word "Binding". For example, in order to bind property x of the foo object to property y of bar object, we would first create one of the objects as shown:

```
MyApp.bar = SC.Object.create({
  y: 'baz'
});
```

Next we would create the binding on our other object as shown:

```
MyApp.foo = SC.Object.create({
  x: 'baz',
  xBinding: SC.Binding.from('MyApp.bar.y')
});
```

In this example, xBinding creates a binding between the x and y properties of the two objects.

Note that we also pre-defined the x property in `MyApp.foo`, while not strictly necessary here, it's a good habit to follow. Otherwise the initial value of x would be `undefined`, and the binding would have to synchronize once initially to `baz` from `undefined`.

There is a short form for writing bindings using only the path string for the value (for example, "MyApp.bar.y"), but the reason it is good to use the long form version is that the short form only translates to `SC.Binding.from`, which relays changes in both directions.

However, more often we have one root object that owns the property and all other bound objects just want to get but not set the property. If you think back to the **Hubbub** example described earlier, none of those five highlighted areas needed to set the `isBorrowed` property, they just needed to be updated when the object changes.

Therefore, in this common situation it is a good idea to use the slightly more efficient unidirectional version of `SC.Binding`, which has no short form as shown:

```
xBinding: SC.Binding.oneWay('MyApp.bar.y')
```

Now whenever y changes, x will be updated to match, but changing x directly would not update y.

So what do we do if we want x to be dependent on y, but not exactly the same value as y? One option is that we could make a computed property. For example:

```
MyApp.bar = SC.Object.create({
  y: 'baz'
});

MyApp.foo = SC.Object.create({

  x:'baz',
  xBinding: 'MyApp.bar.y',

  displayX: function () {
    var x = this.get('x');

    return x.toUpperCase();
  }.property('x').cacheable()

});
```

This works, but it's possible to do it with less code using a "binding transform". To create a transform, we chain the `transform` function to the binding. For example:

```
MyApp.foo = SC.Object.create({

  displayX: 'Baz',
  displayXBinding: SC.Binding.oneWay('MyApp.bar.y').transform(
    function (value) {
      return value.toUpperCase();
    }
  )
});
```

There are several pre-built binding transforms that you can use within SproutCore:

- `bool()`: This forces the value to be boolean `true` or `false` (`null`, `undefined`, and `0` are all `false`).

- `single()`: This forces the value to be a single value. Arrays with a single item will return that item, arrays with multiple items will return `SC.MULTIPLE_PLACEHOLDER`.

- `multiple()`: This forces the value to be an array-like object. Single items will be wrapped in an array.

- `notEmpty()`: This forces the value to not be empty. Values of `null`, `undefined`, `''`, and `[]` will return `SC.EMPTY_PLACEHOLDER`.

- `notNull()`: This forces the value to not be `null`. Values of `null` and `undefined` will return `SC.EMPTY_PLACEHOLDER`. Values of `''` and `[]` are untouched.

- `not()`: This forces the value to be the inverse boolean. This is the same as `bool()`, but inverted.

- `isNull()`: This forces the value to be `true` if the original value is `null` or `undefined`, otherwise the value will be `false`.

Just as we did with the custom transform above, we can chain transforms together to finely tune the resulting value. For example:

```
// Takes a selection array and returns true if there is only one
item and it is truthy
isFirstItemValidBinding: SC.Binding.oneWay('MyApp.listController.
selection').single().bool()
```

Finally, just like with observers, you can manually connect and disconnect bindings on the fly, but this is a rarely used pattern and beyond the scope of this book. For now, everything we've learned so far is all we need to build production worthy applications.

Working with enumerables

In this section we will look at some useful additions SproutCore provides when working with collections. But first, what do we mean by enumerables? In computing science, enumerables are typically the additions to a collection type that provide useful functions for traversing, searching, filtering, and performing operations on the collection's items. In JavaScript, we have two collection types: Object ({}) and Array ([]). But while the latest version of ECMAScript defines several "enumerable" methods for accessing, manipulating, and iterating over JavaScript arrays, actual support for these methods in the various browser implementations is varied.

As such, one of the convenient extensions that SproutCore provides is the `SC.Enumerable` mixin. Any object that mixes in `SC.Enumerable` becomes an "enumerable", which is to say, that the object's contents, ordered or unordered, can be accessed, manipulated, and iterated using a standard interface across all platforms. This means you do not need to worry about a specific JavaScript implementation to use standard methods such as `forEach`, `getEach`, `setEach`, `nextObject`, and others to work with the objects.

There are actually many helper methods that `SC.Enumerable` provides, such as `map`, `reduce`, and `some` but we will just look at a couple of the basic methods here and you should refer to the online documentation for more details.

> The `SC.Enumerable` interface is based primarily off of the ECMAScript 5 Array definitions and in cases where the browser provides the function natively, `SC.Enumerable` will defer to the native version, which will be faster. The difference between the ECMAScript definition and `SC.Enumerable` is that `SC.Enumerable` can also be used on unordered collections, and of course using `SC.Enumerable` ensures that SproutCore apps will still function on the thousands of older browsers out there. Another difference and perhaps the most important one, is that enumerables are **Key-value observing (KVO)** aware so that changes to the enumerable's content will trigger observers and bindings.

The first thing to know is that while you can create your own enumerable collection classes, SproutCore already includes a few basic ones in the runtime environment: SC.Array ([]), SC.Set, and SC.IndexSet. SC.IndexSet is used for tracking ranges of indexes against large collections and we won't look at it specifically in this book. We will however look briefly at SC.Array and SC.Set right now.

SC.Array

SC.Array is the strangest of the enumerables, in that it's not actually a class but an extension to the SC.Enumerable mixin for ordered collections. In terms of using a plain SC.Array instance, it is actually applied to the native JavaScript array object, which is why I wrote SC.Array ([]) earlier. Therefore to use SC.Array, we just use regular JavaScript arrays. For example:

```
// Creating SC.Array instances in SproutCore
var x = ['a', 'b', 'c'];
var y = [];
```

As you can see, there is nothing particularly special about the arrays on the surface. However there are two important points. The first is that we now have access to all of the helper methods of SC.Enumerable and SC.Array. For example, we can use getEach and setEach for simple deep property access as shown in the following screenshot:

The other important point is that we also have access to the KVO-aware methods of SC.Array, which allows us to bind and observe the array attributes and be notified when the array is manipulated. We will look at this in more detail in a moment.

SC.Set

This enumerable-based class is used for unordered collections of items. Similarly to how SC.Array extends the regular JavaScript array, SC.Set can be thought of as an extension over a regular JavaScript object acting as an unordered collection of items. However, SC.Set is not applied to the regular JavaScript object, it is a class and you have to create an instance to use it.

Here is a small introductory example of working with sets. In this example, we create an SC.Set instance and use the SC.Enumerable helper, forEach, to easily iterate through the items.

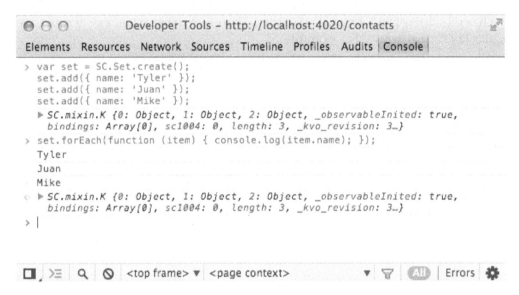

Observing enumerables

As I've alluded to a couple times already, the main reason for SC.Enumerable and SC.Array is the addition of KVO-aware methods that allow us to be notified when the enumerable's content changes. Let's look at arrays first.

The following KVO-aware methods are added to the regular JavaScript array: pushObject, pushObjects, shiftObject, shiftObjects, removeObject, removeObjects, removeAt, replace, and insertAt. Therefore, if you are mutating an array and you want to ensure that KVO works, you must be sure to use one of these methods.

Here's an example observing the `length` property of an array for changes. Be sure to pay attention to how the KVC manipulations actually trigger the observer function to run.

Notice that the array actually notifies that length has changed when calling replace. This is actually a missing optimization with the implementation of `replace` in `SC.Array` that will likely get fixed in the future. Therefore we should not observe the `length` property to be notified when the contents of the array have changed.

So what should we observe, if it's possible to mutate a collection without changing its length? As it turns out, `SC.Enumerable` provides a special property `[]` exactly for this purpose, which we will call the "enumerable" property. By observing the enumerable property, we can be sure to be notified when the contents of the enumerable object change.

Let's look at another example, this time observing the enumerable property [] on an `SC.Set` instance.

```
○ ○ ○          Developer Tools – http://localhost:4020/contacts
Elements  Resources  Network  Sources  Timeline  Profiles  Audits │ Console
> var set = SC.Set.create();

  set.addObserver('[]', function () {
    console.log('content changed');
  });
  ▶ SC.mixin.K {_observableInited: true, bindings: Array[0], _kvo_cloned:
    Object, _kvo_observers_[]: SC.ObserverSet.constructor,
    _kvo_observed_keys: SC.mixin.K…}
> set.add('a');
  content changed
  ▶ SC.mixin.K {0: "a", _observableInited: true, bindings: Array[0],
    _kvo_cloned: Object, _kvo_observers_[]: SC.ObserverSet.constructor,
    _kvo_observed_keys: SC.mixin.K…}
> set.addEach(['b', 'c', 'd']);
  content changed
  ▶ SC.mixin.K {0: "a", 1: "d", 2: "c", 3: "b", _observableInited: true,
    bindings: Array[0], _kvo_cloned: Object, _kvo_observers_[]:
    SC.ObserverSet.constructor, _kvo_observed_keys: SC.mixin.K…}
> set.remove('c')
  content changed
  ▶ SC.mixin.K {0: "a", 1: "d", 2: "b", _observableInited: true, bindings:
    Array[0], _kvo_cloned: Object, _kvo_observers_[]:
    SC.ObserverSet.constructor, _kvo_observed_keys: SC.mixin.K…}

>

  □  ⟩Ξ  ⚲  ⊘  <top frame> ▼  <page context>         ▼  ▽  Ⓐ │ Errors  ⚙
```

As you can see, by observing [] we are properly notified of each change to the contents of the set. Here is the full list of SC.Set's KVO-aware methods: `add`, `addEach`, `pop`, `remove`, and `removeEach`.

Observing properties on enumerable items

We already saw that we can observe the [] property of an enumerable to be notified when objects are added and removed from the enumerable, but what about being notified when an individual object's properties change? Have a look at the following example:

In this example, the observer function is never called. This is because while the internal property of the first item changed, it is still the same object as far as the `people` array is concerned.

To add a deep observer to each item of the array, we use a special property path containing `@each`. By including `@each` in the path after an array property, SproutCore will automatically observe the property path on each item in the array. Let's try that example again but with an observer using an `@each` property path:

As you can see, by using @each.name, our observer function runs when the content membership changes as well as when the name property of any item changes.

 Like with all observers, @each should be used only when necessary as it requires additional processing to set up, run, and tear down.

Understanding the run loop

The last topic of the runtime environment is the run loop. The run loop is an extremely important adaptation that makes SproutCore outperform other frameworks and makes it possible to achieve incredible performance in a web app in spite of the many constraints of the browser. The reason I haven't talked much about the run loop before this point is because as a developer you generally don't need to think about the run loop and I don't want anyone to get into the habit of trying to manipulate the run loop timing without first fully understanding what they're doing.

For most projects, you should be able to ignore the run loop entirely simply by always using SproutCore technologies that are already run loop aware. This includes using SC.Request for XHR, using SC.Timer for timers and using SC.Event for custom event handling for example. But in case that you do need to create a new run loop aware event handler or adjust the execution timing of some code, I will give you a brief overview of the function of the run loop.

In SproutCore there is actually only a single run loop, which is idle until a "run" is triggered. All of the standard document events like 'mousedown', 'touchstart', 'keydown', and so on, will trigger a run of the run loop, as will the asynchronous event handlers in the previously mentioned SC.Request and SC.Timer classes.

When the run loop runs, it coordinates code execution so that by the end of the run loop all the changes from our asynchronous event have flushed through bindings across the entire application and the display has updated if necessary. This describes two very important features of the run loop. The first is that at the end of the run loop the state of our application is synchronized, which is a deeply important point that I can't do justice to enough in such a short section, but by keeping the "truth" inside the code and not in the DOM, our user interface will always be in sync and we have made a gigantic leap ahead in our ability to deliver complex applications. The second feature is that SproutCore coordinates any display updates to the end of the current run loop. For example, if a property that affects the display changes 100 times in one pass, SproutCore only ever updates the display once with the final value.

Now while we should almost never need to manually trigger a run of the run loop, if your app is handling non-standard events not covered by SproutCore (for example, the IndexedDB or WebSQL events) then you must take care to start the run loop in order to flush the updates across the app.

To execute code within a run loop, simply wrap it within `SC.run()`. For example, a `websocket` message event handler would look as shown:

```
// …
socket.on('message', function (message) {
  SC.run( function () {
    // Start a run of the run loop so any changes made here
propagate
    // …
  });
});
// …
```

Again, the above example is a rare occurrence, only to be used when handling non-standard events that are not already handled by SproutCore.

Lastly, there are also functions provided by the run loop that allow you to invoke blocks of code in a certain execution order. Here are the four methods and a description of when you may want to use each:

- `invokeOnce(func)`: This invokes the given function only once in the current run. This is useful if a function can potentially be called from multiple places, but you want to ensure it only runs once.

- `invokeLast(func)`: This invokes the given function only once at the end of the loop after bindings have flushed and after the views have updated. This is useful if the function relies on the final value of bindings or the rendered view output.

- `invokeNext(func)`: This invokes the given function only once asynchronously immediately following the end of the current run loop. This is useful to defer certain expensive functions until after the browser has a chance to break JavaScript execution and repaint and reflow.

- `invokeLater(func, interval)`: This invokes the given function only once at some time later as determined by the `interval` argument. This is useful to delay execution of a function for some time and still coordinate execution with the run loop rather than using `setTimeout`.

While we can call these methods directly on the current run loop object, which is always accessible via `SC.RunLoop.currentRunLoop`, it's easiest to use the same named convenience wrappers from `SC.Object`. For example, calling `myObject.invokeLast()` on an `SC.Object` instance.

 Do not use `invokeLater` to fix apparent timing problems with your code! Any timing issues that occur are likely the result of improper use of computed properties, bindings, and observers and so you should review your code first. As a rule, `invokeLater` shouldn't be used with an interval of less than 200 ms. Otherwise, it's not really "later" in terms of how long the current block of code may possibly take to execute.

Summary

This brings us to the conclusion of the runtime environment. You should now be prepared to create your own `SC.Object` subclasses to organize your code and use mixins to avoid overly rigid hierarchies and code duplication. You should also know how to define properties and computed properties for your objects and how to access them correctly using key-value coding so that the observers and bindings that you create will all work together for simple, fast and error-free code.

This was a fairly in depth look at SproutCore's runtime and indeed gives us everything we need to write a complete SproutCore application. But there is still a lot more that SproutCore offers to make application development easier. As you learn more and try it out yourself, be sure to revisit some of the sections in this chapter to refresh your understanding of the fundamentals often. In particular, I've included important tips for using computed properties, observers and bindings, which I believe make for easier to maintain and more fundamentally correct code.

Hopefully before too long, this will all become second nature to you and you can begin to create even more advanced patterns on top of this powerful platform.

In the next chapter we will look at the MVC pattern in SproutCore and we will look specifically at the View component of that in great detail. This includes all aspects of working with SproutCore views as well as the role of the views in a SproutCore application.

3
The View Layer

In the next few chapters, we will closely look at each of the three layers in the standard **Model-View-Controller (MVC)** model as it is implemented in SproutCore. In this chapter, we will first go through the basic arrangement of the MVC layers at a high level, including the additional layers required for building web software, that are missing from the basic MVC definition.

We will also look at the View layer with significant detail, including how to organize and build views as well as how to render, update, and style them.

In this chapter, we will cover the following:

- MVC in SproutCore
- Understanding the View layer
- Becoming familiar with `SC.View` and `SC.Pane`
- Organizing panes using `SC.Page`
- Laying out views
- Styling views
- Rendering custom views
- Updating custom views
- Responding to user events in custom views

MVC in SproutCore

Before we closely look at the View layer, we should take a moment to understand SproutCore's MVC architecture. I use the term MVC here more often for the pattern's familiarity to most developers than for any other hard and fast interpretation because, the important part of the theory isn't the names or arrangements of the layers as much as it is the idea of *separation of concerns*.

Therefore, I'd rather not spend much time trying to theorize the differences between client-side and server-side MVC, or between MVC and **Model-View-View-Model (MVVM)**, or some other arrangement. Instead, we'll focus only on the role of each MVC layer in SproutCore and how they help us with our main concern, which is writing excellent softwares.

Since SproutCore runs entirely within the client, it does change the dynamics of many things, including the role of the MVC layers. For a quick reference, SproutCore's MVC arrangement closely resembles MVC in the Cocoa framework, but since MVC in any form does not define the entire architecture required for a client-side web application, we will introduce three additional layers: the Display layer, the Application State layer, and the Data Interface layer.

The following is a figure of all the layers in a SproutCore application which shows MVC and these additional layers:

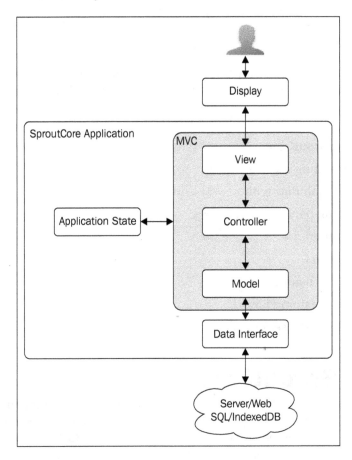

The first new layer is the Display layer, which is essentially the web browser in this case. Unlike a native application, a web application's views cannot paint directly to the screen. Instead, the views' role is to generate the HTML that will be passed to the browser so that the browser can determine what to draw on the screen. This is the case for all web applications and I've drawn it outside the SproutCore Application box because we don't provide this layer ourselves; it is provided by the browser and we simply use it.

The second new layer is actually not specific to web applications and certainly not common to all frameworks, although it should be! I've named this layer Application State, which as the name implies, is the layer responsible for maintaining the state of the application. Every application has an inherent application state, usually mixed somewhere inside the other MVC layers, but in SproutCore we formalize this in its own important layer. We will look at the Application State layer in detail alongside the Controller layer in *Chapter 5, The Controller Layer*.

The final new layer is the Data Interface layer. This layer is responsible for providing data to the Model layer by interfacing with one or more remote data stores. The remote data store may be a server on the Internet or a local IndexedDB database in the client, but regardless of what it is, the Data Interface layer is the one that provides read and write access to it. We will look at the Data Interface layer further alongside the model layer in the next chapter.

Finally, as you must have noticed from the preceding figure, the View layer is stacked upon the Controller layer, which is stacked upon the Model layer. In SproutCore MVC, views do not interact with models directly. Instead, views and models are bound to controllers, which allow the controllers to proxy and transform the data as necessary. We will have a more detailed look on this in *Chapter 5, The Controller Layer*.

Understanding the View layer

The View layer in SproutCore is a powerful and thick layer. In fact, I'm going to start by asserting that the View layer will likely be the most complex layer in your application.

The reason for this being that the View layer has the difficult task of presenting the abstract computational logic and data in a manner both meaningful and easy-to-use for the human being on the other side of the screen. On top of this, it has to work with multiple rendering engines and display sizes and still be fast, smooth, and beautiful.

So, we might as well get comfortable with the idea right now. Designing and developing a **User Interface** (**UI**) is hard work. It requires the web developer to move back and forth between the programmatic language of JavaScript and the semantic languages of HTML and **Cascading Style Sheets** (**CSS**). It requires foresight and nuance and a healthy dose of iteration.

Fortunately for us, SproutCore has done all of the difficult tasks already and so we don't need to worry about things such as optimized rendering, delegating events, handling keystrokes, hardware accelerated animating, and other core view functions. Instead, we can focus more on the configuration and styling of our views and the overall user experience.

This brings me to the two roles of the View layer in SproutCore: to dynamically generate HTML for display and to respond to user events. As mentioned earlier, the View layer interacts with the Display layer by providing HTML for display and we will look at how this is done shortly. What may be new to you though is that the View layer is also the first responder for all user driven events. This means that views receive the mouse, touch, keyboard, and other user events first and can decide to modify them appropriately and/or send the action deeper.

So, unlike a rigid template-based web application, SproutCore views are meant to be dynamic and responsive. Because of this, the user may interact directly with the View layer for some time before the layer needs to pass the user intent down to a lower layer.

Becoming familiar with SC.View and SC.Pane

Unsurprisingly, the View layer is primarily made of objects called views and the base class for all the views in SproutCore is SC.View. SC.View provides the machinery needed to render and update the views' elements. As part of the advanced display requirements of modern apps, SC.View also provides support for hardware accelerated cross browser animations and for being themed, both of which we will look at later.

First, let's look at how to arrange views to create a UI. In SproutCore, views are defined in a tree structure such as the DOM tree structure, where each view has zero or more child views accessible through the childViews property and has one parent view accessible through the parentView property. Each view has a parent view, except for the topmost view in a tree, which is where SC.Pane comes in.

SC.Pane is a special subclass of SC.View that resides at the top of a view tree and is the only type of view that can append and remove itself directly from the DOM. SproutCore provides several pre-built panes for us to use such as SC.MainPane, SC.PanelPane, SC.AlertPane, SC.SheetPane, SC.PickerPane, SC.MenuPane, and SC.PalettePane. As you can tell by the names, most of these panes act as accessory panes to the main interface. The exception to this is the SC.MainPane, which acts as the main interface pane. Every SproutCore application should have one main pane attached, which will house the main views for the current application state.

Only one main pane may be attached at a time and if in case you append another, SproutCore will remove the former. However, you may append as many of the accessory type panes as you like.

Let's look at an example of a basic SproutCore pane and the view hierarchy. The following is a sample wireframe of a pane we want to create:

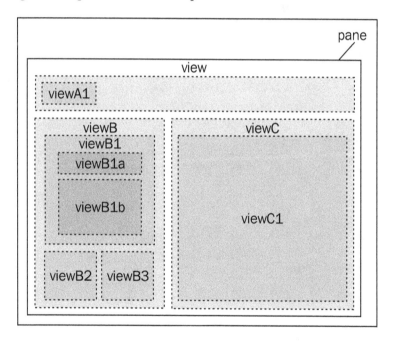

Whether we think of each box as an HTML div or a SproutCore view does not matter as the resulting structure is identical. In order to define all of these views in SproutCore, we arrange the code to match the same hierarchy ('view' contains 'viewA', 'viewB', and 'viewC'; 'viewA' contains 'viewA1'; and so on).

For example:

```
var pane = SC.Pane.create({
  childViews: ['view'],

  view: SC.View.extend({
    childViews: ['viewA', 'viewB', 'viewC'],

    viewA: SC.View.extend({
      childViews: ['viewA1'],

      viewA1: SC.View
    }),

    viewB: SC.View.extend({
      childViews: ['viewB1', 'viewB2', 'viewB3'],

      viewB1: SC.View.extend({
        childViews: ['viewB1a', 'viewB1b'],

        viewB1a: SC.View,

        viewB1b: SC.View
      }),

      viewB2: SC.View,

      viewB3: SC.View
    }),

    viewC: SC.View.extend({
      childViews: ['viewC1'],

      viewC1: SC.View
    })
  })

});
```

As you can see, the `childViews` array for each view contains the names of the children for that view, which are properties on the same view. As each view is created, it will look up all the named child views in `childViews` and create them too. As each child view is created, its `parentView` property will be set, thus connecting the entire tree.

You will undoubtedly encounter examples of view trees using `design` and `extend` interchangeably. For all intensive purposes, these can be considered to be the same method. The `design` method is really just `extend`, along with indicating that the view should be loadable in a designer application for modification using a GUI tool. While work on an **Integrated Development Environment (IDE)** for SproutCore has progressed, no usable product exists yet. Therefore, the `design` method remains available till the time an IDE is completed.

We can then access any particular view using property paths. For example, to get `viewB1`, we would use the following code line:

```
var viewB1 = pane.getPath('view.viewB.viewB1');
```

And if we want to access `viewB` from within `viewB1a`, we would use the following code line:

```
var view = this.getPath('parentView.parentView');
```

You will probably feel this approach using view property paths is a bit ugly and you are correct! I only mention it for reference sake, because we should generally avoid searching out views in this way and instead, *use bindings to pass configuration changes directly to the views.*

Finally, we can also dynamically modify the arrangement of views using the manipulation methods of `SC.View`: `appendChild`, `insertBefore`, `removeChild`, `replaceChild`, and `replaceAllChildren`. The following screenshot is an example of adding and removing child views dynamically using the previous pane:

```
Developer Tools - http://localhost:4020/my_app

Elements  Resources  Network  Sources  Timeline  Profiles  Audits  Console

> view = pane.get('view');
  view.get('childViews').getEach('layerId');  // There are three child views
  ["sc790", "sc792", "sc798"]
> viewB = view.get('viewB');
  viewB.get('layerId'); // viewB is the middle child view
  "sc792"
> view.removeChild(viewB);
  view.get('childViews').getEach('layerId');  // viewB has been removed
  ["sc790", "sc798"]
> viewA = view.get('viewA');
  viewA.get('layerId'); // viewA is the first child view
  "sc790"
> view.insertBefore(viewB, viewA);
  view.get('childViews').getEach('layerId');  // viewB is now the first child view
  ["sc792", "sc790", "sc798"]
>

        Q  ⊘  <top frame> ▼  All  |  Errors  Warnings  Logs  Debug
```

Organizing panes using SC.Page

Since an application may have several different preconfigured panes and pages (that is, subclasses of SC.Pane), we need a means to organize them all. This is the purpose of the SC.Page object. But don't let the name confuse you. SC.Page is not a type of SC.View and has nothing to do with rendering the visual page. It is simply a storage object used to hold preconfigured but un-instantiated panes and views.

Using an SC.Page container gives your application an anchor point for looking up a particular view tree and retrieving it for use. This is convenient, but the real work of the page container is that it will only instantiate objects when they are accessed the first time, allowing you to avoid creating all your panes at launch or defining classes that would be wasted with only one instance. I realize that this idea may be a bit abstract right now, so let's look at an example.

Here's the skeleton of a file that will represent the login page for an application. It contains the main page (mainPane) and a panel for creating a new account (createAccountPane). You can imagine that these two panes would eventually contain several predefined views, but for now I've left them empty.

```
log_in_page.js
1   MyApp.logInPage = SC.Page.create({
2
3     mainPane: SC.MainPane.extend({
4       // Contains several views such as labels and fields.
5       // ...
6     }),
7
8     createAccountPane: SC.PanelPane.extend({
9       // A panel we use for creating a new account.
10      // ...
11    })
12
13  });
```

Line 11, Column 5   Spaces: 2   JavaScript

So, why put these inside an SC.Page file? Well as I mentioned previously, MyApp.logInPage is a singleton, which allows you to easily access the page anywhere within the application. What we will encounter later is that we will likely have a login state that will work in sync with this pane, appending it as the state is entered.

For example:

```
// entering log in state
MyApp.logInPage.get('mainPane').append();
```

Likewise, if the user clicks on a **Create Account** button, we would want to handle that by appending the pane returned by MyApp.logInPage. get('createAccountPane').

The next point I made about how using SC.Page is better than a singleton or a class, is a bit more difficult to describe. So, let's look at what happens when I play around with logInPage in the browser's console:

Let me walk you through the previous example. First, I accessed the mainPane property using dot notation, which is against key-value coding principles, but I did so to prove a point. When I used dot notation the first time, we see that MyApp. logInPage.mainPane is an SC.MainPane class. This means that the pane has not been instantiated and we haven't paid the setup cost required to connect bindings and observers. In fact, if we never use this pane, it will never get instantiated, saving on processing and memory. This is better than using a singleton for the mainPane, which would have been created when the file would have been parsed, hampering the performance at launch.

Next, I accessed the mainPane property properly using get and we see that SC.Page instantiated the object for me. Finally, I accessed the property again using dot notation just to check and we see that something interesting has happened. The class has now been replaced by the instance. This is a subtle feature, but because there is only ever one mainPane, we don't need to keep the class around and so SC.Page replaces it, freeing up a bit of memory.

Page files should reside in the application's **Resources** directory. I will usually put each main pane in its own page, such as `main_page.js`, `log_in_page.js`, and so on. If there are a lot of accessory panes or they are complex, you may want to split them into multiple `SC.Page` containers across multiple files too.

Laying out views

Now that we have our views organized, let's look at the layout of each of them. SproutCore views are absolutely positioned by default, which is easiest to work with for full-screen applications and also faster due to the fact that the browser doesn't need to reflow the entire page when a portion changes.

To position and size our views, we use the `layout` property. This property is used by SproutCore to assign a layout style to a view's element when it is rendered. While we could lay out everything with CSS, this requires more back and forth movement in between files and would separate our view code from the size and position information. Instead, by programmatically defining the layout, we keep the truth about our view's layout inside the code, which allows us to avoid going to the DOM to measure elements when we need to adjust or animate them. Remember, in order to keep our web application fast, we need to avoid touching the DOM unless absolutely necessary.

The following are all the possible layout attributes we can use: `top`, `left`, `bottom`, `right`, `centerX`, `centerY`, `width`, `height`, `minWidth`, `maxWidth`, `minHeight`, `maxHeight`, `border`, `borderTop`, `borderLeft`, `borderBottom`, `borderRight`, `opacity`, and `zIndex`. Obviously, we can't use all of these attributes at the same time because some of them would conflict with each other. For example, you can't use `width` at the same time with both `left` and `right` because that doesn't make logical sense. SproutCore will warn us if we try to do something improper like this.

To define a layout, simply set the property to a regular JavaScript object. The default layout is `{ top: 0, left: 0, bottom: 0, right: 0 }` and SproutCore is smart about implied layouts. So, you don't need to define each property every time.

Following are a few example layouts to get you started. The resulting layout style is shown in the comment before the property.

```
a: SC.LabelView.extend({
  // style="height: 150px; right: 0px; left: 0px; top: 0px;"
  layout: { height: 150 },
  value: 'A'
})
```

```
b: SC.LabelView.extend({
  // style="right: 0px; width: 240px; top: 0px; bottom: 0px;"
  layout: { right: 0, width: 240 },
  value: 'B'
})

c: SC.LabelView.extend({
  // style="left: 50%; margin-left: -100px; top: 50%; margin-top:
-100px; height: 200px; width: 200px; "
  layout: { centerX: 0, centerY: 0, height: 200, width: 200 },
  value: 'C'
})

d: SC.LabelView.extend({
  // style="bottom: 20px; left: 50%; margin-left: -38%; height: 40%;
width: 75%; min-width: 200px;"
  layout: { bottom: 20, centerX: 0, height: 0.4, width: 0.75,
minWidth: 200 },
  value: 'D'
})
```

You should notice from the resulting styles that layouts have an added benefit of being more compact to write over raw CSS. In the next collection of screenshots, we can see how each of these layouts appears on the page:

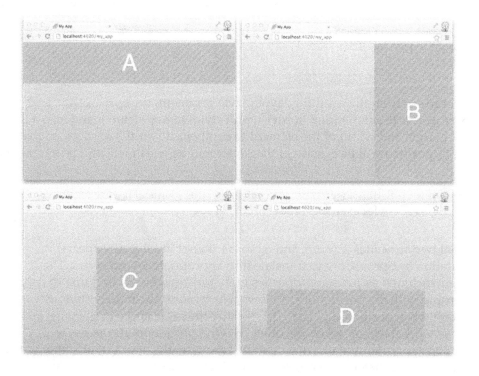

As you can see, we are able to create fairly complex layouts with little typing and these layouts are quite flexible too. For instance, as the window size changes, view **B** will remain anchored to the right, view **C** will remain centered, and view **D** will stay near the bottom and change the width and height.

Speaking of view D, did you notice that its layout specified percentages for `width` and `height`? With the `layout` property, any value between 0.01 and 0.99 will result in a style between 1% and 99% accordingly. There is no need for a 0% or 100% style, because a `height` or `width` of 0 is 0%, a `top` and `bottom` of 0 is a `height` of 100%, and a `left` and `right` of 0 is a `width` of 100%.

Before we move on, we should discuss the other layout properties. First, since borders are added by the browser *outside* the element's content frame, if an element has a layout height of 100 pixels (px) and a 1px top and bottom border in CSS, the actual height of the element would become 102px. By not accounting for borders in layout, we would find our views to be slightly of the wrong size and position. Instead, by setting the border layout attributes, SproutCore will ensure that the position and size of the view is exactly what you specify. Here's view C with a `left` and `right` border:

```
c: SC.LabelView.extend({
  // style="border-left-width: 1px; border-right-width: 3px; left:
50%; margin-left: -98px; top: 50%; margin-top: -100px; height: 200px;
width: 196px; "
  layout: { borderLeft: 1, borderRight: 3, centerX: 0, centerY: 0,
height: 200, width: 200 },
  value: 'C'
})
```

As you can see from the resulting layout style comment, the `borderLeft` and `borderRight` attributes added border width styles to our element and also adjusted the left margin and width of the element to compensate for the borders, so that the element's position will be exactly in the center and its width will still be 200px total.

Setting just the `border` attribute adds identical border width styles to all four sides.

The final two attributes, `zIndex` and `opacity` do not involve any special computation by SproutCore to translate into appropriate layout styles. They are likely included as `layout` properties more for convenience and due to their relationship with the positioning of views. The `zIndex` attribute is obviously important when positioning views that occupy the same space in the page and we want one to be above or below the other. Having programmatic access to `zIndex` allows us to easily shuffle views on the fly. Likewise, the `opacity` attribute is also relevant to views that are overlapping and it's easier to adjust by being in the layout.

Finally, you can always let the browser flow the view elements by setting
`useStaticLayout` to `true` on the view. If `useStaticLayout` is `true`, the view
will not receive the `position: absolute;` style making it easier to position and
size through a CSS layout. While not recommended because of the performance
implications, this is useful for the kind of content that needs to flow naturally such
as long form text.

> Once you switch to relative positioning for a view's layout, you
> can't switch back to absolute positioning for any of its child views
> and may find yourself spending a lot of energy updating style
> sheets and measuring elements. Therefore, you should try to only
> use static layout on views at the bottom of the view hierarchy
> which don't have any child views.

Adjusting the layout

After the layout of a view is set, you can still very easily adjust it programmatically
using the `adjust` method.

For example, calling `adjust('top', 140)` on view A from the previous diagram
would move it instantly as shown in the following screenshot:

Animating the layout

Often, it's a nicer visual experience to animate a change rather than instantly update it. In SproutCore, we can very easily animate the layout adjustments using the `animate` method. For example, the same adjustment from the previous one could be carried out smoothly through the following code line:

```
MyApp.mainPage.getPath('mainPane.viewA').animate('top', 140, {
  duration: 0.3 });
```

In order to use `animate`, we have to provide an optional object to specify how the animation should occur. You must always provide the `duration` value in seconds and can optionally include the timing function, `timing`, or the delay value, `delay`. You can also animate multiple layout properties at the same time, by passing a hash of key value pairs.

For example:

```
myView.animate({ 'top': 100, 'height': 200 }, { duration: 0.7 });
```

You can also include a callback for when the animation completes, by passing a `function` or a target and method as the final arguments to `animate`.

For example:

```
aView.animate('left', -200, { duration: 0.5 }, function () {
  // Do something when the view is done animating.
});
```

 SproutCore will try to use hardware-accelerated CSS transforms for animation whenever possible. Assuming that the browser supports CSS transforms, you can ensure that your animations are hardware-accelerated by only animating the `top` and `left` layout properties of fixed `height` and `width` views that have `wantsAcceleratedLayer` set to `true`.

Styling views

At this point, we have laid out all our views according to how we want them to appear on the page and so, we can begin to look at styling them appropriately. There are three properties on `SC.View` that are useful for styling: `classNames`, `tagName`, and `layerId`.

First, we use the `classNames` property of the view to name one or more CSS class names that the view element will include. For example, to have the classes `title-view` and `blue` included as class names, we would add the following code lines:

```
titleView: SC.View.extend({
  // <div class="title-view blue …
  classNames: ['title-view', 'blue']
}),
```

It is a bit surprising though if you inspected the `class` attribute of the resulting element. You would find it doesn't just contain only the `title-view` and `blue` class names. Here is what it would be for an application called `MyApp`:

```
class="ace my-app sc-view title-view blue"
```

The first two classes `ace` and `my-app` are the result of themes applied by default at the application level. The application's themes add class names to every view and are used to create sets of reusable styles that can be shared across applications. Creating themes is an advanced topic beyond the scope of this book and we will simply override the default SproutCore theme as necessary to style our elements.

The `sc-view` class is included because the `classNames` property is a concatenated property of `SC.View`. Since `SC.View`'s `classNames` array is already `sc-view`, calling `extend` on `SC.View` in this case results in a concatenated `classNames` array of `sc-view`, `title-view`, and `blue`.

The second property that we can modify for styling is the `tagName` property. This is the name of the HTML tag that will be used for the view's element and its default value is `div`. We can set this property to a different HTML tag in order to generate more semantic tags for our view elements.

For example:

```
contentView: SC.View.extend({
  // <section class="body faded …
  classNames: ['body', 'faded'],
  tagName: 'section'
})
```

Finally, you may also specify the ID attribute of your view's element by setting the `layerId` property. I have mentioned this last because it was historically frowned upon to use `layerId` at all. What happens is when `layerId` is undefined, SproutCore generates a unique value for each view, which it uses to map between the view object and its DOM element. If you were careless and created two views with the same `layerId` value, SproutCore would be unable to properly manage the elements for both these views, possibly leading to leftover elements in the DOM and a strange behavior.

However, as of SproutCore 1.10, I've added a warning message that will notify the developer when multiple views use the same `layerId` value, which should make it quite easy to avoid this mistake in the future. Therefore, I see no reason not to set the `layerId` value for your singleton views if you want to style by ID (which is faster than by class). Just be sure that you never have two instances of a class with the same `layerId` value.

For example:

```
headerView: SC.View.extend({
  // <header id="main-header" class="page-header ...
  classNames: ['page-header'],
  layerId: 'main-header',
  tagName: 'header'
}),
```

So to wrap up, we have a few options with regards to how to identify the view's layer so that we can style it through CSS. You will most likely already have a CSS approach that works for you, so I will just give you these additional tips that I find useful. The first thing to know is that Sass (`http://sass-lang.com`) and Compass framework (`http://compass-style.org`) are built into the SproutCore build tools, allowing you to use SCSS syntax and all the Compass mixins to write clean and cross-browser compatible CSS. Using these tools will make your style sheets much more compact and readable and so, you should definitely research on how to use them, if you don't already know.

The second tip is to not be afraid of creating multiple style sheet files. In fact, each page file should likely have a matching style sheet file in the resources directory (for example, `main_page.js` and `main_page.css`) and a view file as well (for example, `custom_label_view.js` and `custom_label_view.css`). Since SproutCore's build tools will concatenate these files into a single style sheet for optimal loading, it doesn't matter how many files we use.

You can also use the `sc_require` pre-processor command inside the style sheets to alter their load order. So, you may want to create a single style sheet with SCSS mixins and variables and require it before your other style sheets.

Let's look at a full example of how we may style a simple heading view. The following examples are the relevant contents of the files we would use.

In `my_app/resources/main_page.js`:

```
// This page describes the main user interface for your application.
MyApp.mainPage = SC.Page.create({

  mainPane: SC.MainPane.extend({
    childViews: ['headingView'],

    headingView: SC.View.extend({
      // <header ...
      tagName: 'header',

      // ... id="heading-view" ...   (This must be unique!)
      layerId: 'heading-view',

      // ... class="sc-view white-text shadowed" ...
      classNames: ['white-text', 'shadowed'],

      // ... style="height: 55px; top: 0px; right: 0px; left: 0px;">
      layout: { height: 55 }

    })
  })

});
```

In `my_app/resources/style_guide.css`:

```
// Include the Compass CSS3 mixins.
@import "compass/css3";

// Common shadowing for divs.
.sc-view.shadowed {
  // Compass has powerful mixins to save us time.
  @include box-shadow(rgba(0,0,0,0.5) 2px 2px 5px);
  overflow: visible;        // .sc-view hides overflow by default
}

// Common white text for dark backgrounds.
.white-text {
  color: white;
  text-shadow: rgba(0,0,0,0.3) 0 1px 2px;
}
```

And in my_app/resources/main_page.css:

```
// We can use sc_require inside of stylesheets to determine the load
order.
// Requiring style_guide.css means that the Compass mixins are
available here now too.
sc_require('resources/style_guide.css');

// SCSS variables makes it easy to quickly tweak styles.
$heading-height: 55px;

// The heading view.
#heading-view {
  @include background-image(linear-gradient(top, #c13400, #982900));
  line-height: $heading-height;
}
```

Rendering custom views

In this section, we will look at the rendering process for SproutCore views. Updating the DOM is one of the slowest points in a web application and so, there are some very important steps that SproutCore uses to avoid touching the DOM unnecessarily. While all of the pre-built SproutCore views are already written to take full advantage of this, when we do custom rendering, it's important that we understand the render cycle in order to keep our views fast. Don't worry; it's not difficult to follow and you will have no problem creating complex views by the time we're done with this chapter.

We've already discussed how to affect the view's top level element by setting layerId, tagName, classNames, and layout but we haven't yet discussed how to create custom inner content for the element. To do so, there are two methods in SC.View that we use: render and update. The render method is called the first time the view is displayed and update is called each time the view's display changes.

Let's look at the render method first. Its job is to generate the HTML string to be passed to the Display layer and it does this using a simple HTML string builder called SC.RenderContext. Let's start by creating a custom label view class, NameLabelView, for our fictional application, MyApp:

In my_app/views/name_label_view.js:

```
MyApp.NameLabelView = SC.View.extend({

  /** The name. */
```

```
    name: '',

    /** @private Generates the view element's content.

      @param SC.RenderContext context the string builder object.
    */
    render: function (context) {
      var name = this.get('name');

      // Add a "Name:" label along with the name.
      context.push('<label class="name-label">Name: </label><span>' +
name + '</span>');
    }
});
```

As you can see, to render this view, all we do is push a `Name:` label term followed by the current value of `name` into the render context we are given. The `push` method simply adds the given string to the context, unaltered.

While you can use `push` a lot of the time, the render context does have more declarative methods that we can use to build the output. Here is the same `render` method using a series of build commands:

```
render: function (context) {
  var name = this.get('name');

  // Add a "Name:" label.
  context = context.begin('label')
    .addClass('name-label')
    .push("Name: ")
    .end();

  // Add the name.
  context = context.begin('span').push(name).end();
}
```

This time we used `begin('label')` to start a new sub-context specific to the label element. We set its class using `addClass`, pushed the `Name:` string to it, and closed it off before starting another sub-context for span.

 Along with `addClass`, the other methods you will find useful are `setClass`, `addStyle`, `setStyle`, `addAttr`, and `setAttr`. You can find more information on each of these in the documentation of `SC.RenderContext`.

Now, whenever an instance of `MyApp.NameLabelView` is appended to the document, its `render` function will be called and our custom label will appear in the DOM.

> In order to update DOM most efficiently, when a pane is appended, SproutCore will call the `render` function for every child view recursively, in order to build the entire HTML string at once. The final string will then be inserted into the DOM in a single call, which is significantly faster than building one child view at a time within the DOM.

Updating custom views

The next step in creating a functional custom view is to efficiently update the display when necessary. For instance, in the previous example, we would want to be sure about updating the display each time the value of `name` changes. To do this, we use the `displayProperties` array to name the properties that, when changed, should cause our view's display to update.

Therefore, here's an addition to `MyApp.NameLabelView` that will ensure our view updates each time the `'name'` value changes:

```
MyApp.NameLabelView = SC.View.extend({

    displayProperties: ['name'],

    // ...
```

> Each property named in `displayProperties` will be observed for changes. So, be sure to only list those properties that directly affect the rendering. Listing extra properties wastes processing time and causes unnecessary display updates.

This will actually work as it is using our previous `render` code, but it will not be as efficient as it could be.

In the absence of the `update` method in the view, SproutCore will instead call the `render` method again and replace the entire inner HTML of the element with the regenerated HTML. You can very well imagine that if we generate a lot of HTML in our `render` function, this would not be an optimal way to update only a small portion of it.

Instead, we will implement the `update` method to selectively update only that portion of our view that has changed. For example, this is how we would update only the `name span` part:

```
MyApp.NameLabelView = SC.View.extend({

    displayProperties: ['name'],

    // ...

    /** @private Updates the view element's content.

      @param Object jqElement the jQuery object for the element.
    */
    update: function (jqElement) {
      var name = this.get('name');

      // Update the name span.
      jqElement.find('span').html(name);
    }

});
```

Notice that the `update` method is passed a jQuery object for the element. This makes it easy to quickly find the relevant node and use jQuery's methods to update it. That is all there is to know to render and update your custom SproutCore views.

Because of bindings and the run loop, updating is extremely efficient in SproutCore. If our name property from the previous example depended on several other properties that have all changed, it will not hurt performance. What will happen is that all the bound values will flush back and forth until the final value for the name property is set. Only then will SproutCore call `update`, thus avoiding touching the DOM more than once, even when noisy events occur in the application.

Responding to user events in custom views

One of the most difficult tasks in any software is responding to user events properly. On the surface it may seem trivial, but we quickly find that there are many context-specific variables that need to be considered.

First, there is the matter of efficiently listening to events within a complex and dynamic UI. In SproutCore, we do this via the root responder object, `SC.RootResponder`, which acts as the sole listener for all the user events. Having a single listener is much easier and faster than manually adding the many mouse, touch, keyboard, and other event listeners directly to each element. If we did try to manage the events per view, we would have to write a lot of extra code and in turn, would lose performance and possibly introduce memory leaks as the dynamic UI changes.

Instead, as the sole event listener, `SC.RootResponder` is able to direct events to the proper responder object, which may not necessarily even be a view. The way it works is that each browser event that occurs (mousedown, touchstart, keydown, and so on) has a corresponding action (`mouseDown`, `touchStart`, `keyDown`, and so forth) that can be implemented on a target. If the target implements the action, the event will stop. If the target doesn't implement the action, the event will continue to bubble up to the next responder. In this way, we can create our own responder chains to handle events efficiently.

For our purpose right now, we'll leave the discussion on responder chains since the view responder chain is set up automatically for us and we can simply focus on which actions we want to handle in our custom views. For example, let's create an extremely basic button view that will respond to mouse events:

```
MyApp.MyButtonView = SC.View.extend({

  mouseDown: function (evt) {
    // Indicate that we handled the event.
    return true;
  },

  mouseUp: function (evt) {
    // Perform some action ...

    // Indicate that we handled the event.
    return true;
  }

});
```

That is all there is to it. By implementing `mouseDown` and `mouseUp`, our view's action will be called whenever the user clicks on its element. If we also want to handle other events, such as touch and key presses, we would simply add the appropriate actions (for example, `touchStart`, `touchEnd`, and `keyDown`).

 Be sure to return `true` when handling `mouseDown`. The root responder is conservative and will only call `mouseUp` on the same responder that handled `mouseDown`.

However, as I had alluded in the beginning of this section, handling events and properly handling events are two vastly different things. I'm afraid our simple button view is far too simple to be of much use right now. This is because it's not taking into consideration several other factors such as whether the view was enabled, whether the mouse was dragged out of the element, whether any modifier keys were pressed, or even which mouse button was clicked. For now, you should be aware of the basics and if you want to explore custom view event handling in more depth, you should check out the source code of some of the built-in SproutCore controls such as `SC.ButtonView` and `SC.TextField`.

Summary

That brings us to the end of this chapter. Here, we managed to fit an overview of MVC in SproutCore and nearly the entire View layer. We looked at the arrangement of SproutCore MVC and introduced the Display, Application State, and Data Interface layers, that are inherent to client-side web applications. We looked closely at the View layer in SproutCore and how it interacts with the Display layer to perform two important roles for our application: creating the user interface and responding to user events.

At this point, you should understand most of the features of the `SC.View` class and be ready to create entire UI hierarchies using subclasses of `SC.Pane` with `SC.View`-based child views. You should also know how and why you would use the `SC.Page` objects to organize your pages.

We also looked at the manner in which we configure the position and size of our views using the `layout` property and the manner in which we style our views using CSS in combination with the `classNames` (that is, class attribute), `tagName` (that is, tag type) and `layerId` (that is, ID attribute) properties.

Finally, we looked at how to render and update custom views and had our first introduction with event handling for views. While it will take a bit of practice before you create full custom controls, you now have everything you need to define the entire UI for your SproutCore applications.

In the next chapter, we will look at the model layer in SproutCore MVC and how we retrieve, store, manipulate, and synchronize data within the client for advanced functionality and immediate user feedback.

4
The Model Layer

In this chapter, we will move to the opposite end of the application stack and look at the M or Model layer in SproutCore MVC. As it turns out, the implementation of the Model layer within SproutCore is one of the most impressive and unique features of the framework. This layer provides tools for modeling data, applying business logic, querying data, and synchronizing changes between the server and the client. Hence, we can say that the tools in this layer allow us to load raw data into our application from any remote source and use it in a simple and effective manner.

The first thing to recognize is that because we are creating applications for the web, our software is always in a client-server type of relationship where the actual data is stored separately from the application. Even when using a client-side data store such as IndexedDB or WebSQL, our application must asynchronously interface with the data store the same way it would as though the database were on a remote server somewhere. To fulfill the need of interfacing with a variety of remote sources, SproutCore defines a standard **Application Programming Interface (API)** that we can use to write custom data source adaptors. These adaptors belong to, what I called the Data Interface layer in the previous chapter. We will look at the data source adaptor API in this chapter as well so that you fully understand how to integrate with your own remote data sources.

In this chapter, we will cover the following:

- Understanding the Model and Data Interface layers
- Introducing the data store
- Defining your data model
- Creating custom attribute properties
- Defining record relationships

- Following the life cycle of SC.Record
- Querying the store
- Synchronizing data with a remote data source
- Implementing remote data source adaptors

Understanding the Model and Data Interface layers

As I alluded to in the very first chapter of this book, unavoidable network latency prevents any traditional server-side web application from nearing the performance of a native application. When a web application embeds data into templates on the server and serves them one at a time to the user, the experience will be, at best, okay on the desktop, and, at worst, unusable on mobile.

However, while network latency is unavoidable and worsens as users move away from desktop to mobile, we will still provide an exceptional user experience in web applications that use SproutCore. We saw that SproutCore's View layer takes care of most of this problem by allowing us to run a responsive and feature-rich UI in the client, but it would be all for naught, if we didn't have the means to supply that UI with data.

Thus, this is the role of the Model layer: to acquire, store, and provide data for our application's use. To acquire data, the Model layer interacts with the Data Interface layer to request information from a remote source; to store data, the Model layer places the information in one or more local data stores; and to provide data, the Model layer includes a powerful query language and a complete data modeling structure.

Remember that while not all the data will be ready immediately, we can usually make this unnoticeable to the user by not blocking the UI while data is being synchronized and also by pre-fetching data behind the scenes whenever possible. As an added bonus, since we only need raw data from the server and not entire views, each request and response is as fast as possible.

Introducing the data store

The SproutCore data store acts as the repository for most of the data that we will load into a SproutCore application. While you can have multiple data stores in your application, you will probably use just one for the sake of simplicity. To create a store, we simply create an instance of `SC.Store` and in fact, if you use the command line generator (that is, `sproutcore gen app`), you will find that a store is created for you by default, in the application's `core.js` file.

We typically create the main application store as a property of the application object. For example:

```
MyApp = SC.Application.create({

  // The main application data store, accessible as 'MyApp.store'
  store: SC.Store.create()

});
```

You can think of the store as an in-memory database. So, if you have a good idea of the type of data that belongs to a database, you will likely have a good idea of the appropriate data for the store by now. For example, if you will be retrieving records of users, accounts, messages, or other similar data types that you would store in a database, these records will be a perfect fit for the data store. On the other hand, the same types of data that you would not store in a database are likewise not a good fit for the data store. For example, if you retrieve a session for the current user, it's not necessary to give this object its own record class and push it in the store.

Much like a database, you will start by loading data into the store and use queries to retrieve specific data back for use in the application as and when necessary. However, because the real root data resides in one or more remote data stores, SproutCore's data store is actually optimized to act as a quick access database cache. For instance, the store always provides records to the application immediately when requested, but if that data doesn't currently exist in the store, the records will initially be empty while the store requests more information through the Data Interface layer. When the real data arrives, it will be loaded into the store and the empty records will be updated. Of course, with the power of bindings and observers, the UI will be updated automatically as well.

One important point to bring up early is that data in the store is stored as a collection of simple JavaScript objects that we call data hashes. Data hashes are just deserialized data from the remote source that are loaded directly into the store. I do realize that this is a lot of jargon and these various terms may not mean much to you yet, but hopefully the following figure will help you visualize the system we have been talking about so far.

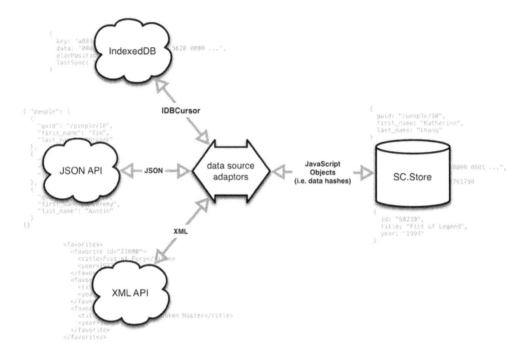

On the left are the remote data sources that provide data to our application and on the right is the application's store. As you can see in the figure, our data source adaptors transform the remote serialized data into simple JavaScript objects (that is, data hashes) that the store will manage.

We will look at how to write data source adaptors at the end of this chapter, but for now it's important just to remember that the data hashes will contain only primitive values such as strings, numbers, and booleans. This is because the data transferred between the application and the remote data sources will likely be in a format such as JSON or XML and so, we benefit by keeping our data hashes in an easily serializeable format.

Next, let's look at the components between the store and the rest of the application.

Defining your data model

When planning the data component of any particular application, we always start with a data model. A data model is just a diagram or description that defines the record types and their relationships. These record types, or models, will closely map the types of data we expect to bring into the application. So, for instance, if we are going to load student record data, we will likely want a `MyApp.Student` model.

Let's look at an example of how a data model for a calendaring application may start out:

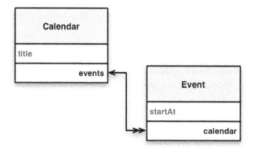

This data model is about as simple as it can get. We have calendar records, each of which has zero or more event records. In turn, each event record has one calendar record. We'll get to coding the record relationships soon, but first we need to be able to define the models and their attributes for our application.

To create record classes we simply extend `SC.Record`.

For example:

```
/** @class
    A calendar record.
*/
MyApp.Calendar = SC.Record.extend({

});

/** @class
    An event in a calendar.
*/
MyApp.Event = SC.Record.extend({

});
```

After creating a record class, the next step is to indicate the attributes of the record. When defining records, we differentiate between the attributes, which are properties backed by the underlying data hash and normal object properties like we learned in the *Chapter 2, The Runtime Environment*.

To define an attribute property for the record, we use an instance of SC.RecordAttribute, which is easily created using the attr helper method of SC.Record. This helper method accepts the type of the attribute as the first argument and a hash of options for the attribute as the second argument.

For example:

```
MyApp.Calendar = SC.Record.extend({

    // Title of the calendar.
    title: SC.Record.attr(String, {
        defaultValue: "New Calendar"
    })

});
```

As you can see in the example, we declared that the title attribute data is of String type and used the defaultValue option to provide a default value for all the newly created MyApp.Calendar records. Because we specified the type as String in this case, when accessing the title value of an individual MyApp.Calendar record, we will get a string value back. This may seem obvious because the attribute in the data hash is most certainly a string itself, but what may not be obvious is how SC.RecordAttribute can transform any simple attribute value into a complex type.

 Besides the String attribute type, SproutCore also includes Number, Boolean, Object, Array, Date, and SC.DateTime attribute types.

Here is an example where the value in the data hash is not of the same type as the value returned by the attribute:

```
/** @class
    An event in a calendar.
*/
MyApp.Event = SC.Record.extend({

    // Start time of the event.
```

```
    startAt: SC.Record.attr(SC.DateTime, {
      format: '%d/%m/%Y %H:%M:%S'
    })

  });
```

In this example, the record's `startAt` property is of type `SC.DateTime`, but the property is just a proxy for the real value in the data hash which will not be of `SC.DateTime` type. Remember that the underlying data hash should only contain directly serializeable values so that we can convert them to JSON, XML, or some other format in order to be sent to the remote data source. In this case, the stored value will be a string and when the `startAt` property is requested, the string from the data hash will be transformed into an `SC.DateTime` object. Likewise, when `startAt` is set to a new `SC.DateTime` object, it will be transformed into a string and stored in the underlying data hash.

Before we continue, there are two common options you should know about when defining attributes. The first is `isEditable`, which, when set to `false`, will prevent the attribute from being changed. If an attribute is not editable, any attempts to modify it on the client will be ignored, which is a useful way to indicate that the remote data store is the only source of truth for certain attributes.

The second option is `key`, which allows you to change the name of the attribute looked up in the underlying data hash. By default, the data hash key is expected to be the same as the property name, but we can use the `key` option in order to name the property one thing and have it backed by an attribute named something else This is useful when the remote data source uses attributes that are unwieldy or don't match the conventions for JavaScript property names. For example, Ruby and Python servers will often use snake case property names (for example, `my_variable`) while most JavaScript programmers prefer camel case (for example, `myVariable`). Although we could rename all the attributes when we deserialize the incoming data or eschew the JavaScript conventions and name our properties to whatever matches the raw data, it's simple enough just to set the appropriate key and so, we often do just that.

For example:

```
// ...

userRole: SC.Record.attr(Number, {

  // This attribute cannot be changed in the client.
  isEditable: false,
```

```
// The actual name of the attribute in the data hash.
key: 'user_role_val'
```

```
})
```

```
// …
```

Finally, there is the matter of an important attribute shared by all records: the primary key. As you probably know, each record in a database must have a unique primary key and SproutCore records in the store are no different. However, the way SC.Record uses primary keys tends to throw people off at first. For one, we do not create an attribute for the primary key of the record. This is because the primary key attribute of all records is already defined by SC.Record and it is id, which is effectively the same as the following:

```
// …
```

```
id: SC.Record.attr(String, {
  key: 'guid'
}),
```

```
// …
```

Therefore, if the primary key name in the data we load is guid, we wouldn't have to make any changes. However, if it is something different, we can change the key used by id by setting the primaryKey property.

For instance, if the primary key attribute in the data for our previous MyApp. Calendar records was _id, our record would look like the following:

```
MyApp.Calendar = SC.Record.extend({

  // Title of the calendar.
  title: SC.Record.attr(String, {
    defaultValue: "New Calendar"
  }),

  // The primary key attribute in the data hash is '_id'.
  primaryKey: '_id'

});
```

Because the `primaryKey` value can be set as per the record class, we can actually work with records loaded from different APIs without having to remember what the specific primary key attribute's name is elsewhere in the application. For example, to get the primary key value of any record we always use the following code line:

```
var id = aRecord.get('id');
```

Creating custom attribute properties

While the built-in `SC.RecordAttribute` transforms, `String`, `Boolean`, `Number`, `Array`, `Object`, `Date`, and `SC.DateTime`, will cover almost all the different types of attributes in your records. If you wish to create a reusable custom transform, this is easily done using `SC.RecordAttribute.registerTransform()`.

For instance, SproutCore provides a class for manipulating colors called `SC.Color`. If we were sending and receiving a lot of color information to and from a remote data source, it would be nice to add a custom transform so that we could use a color string in the data hash for communicating with the server, but use an `SC.Color` object in the record for use in the application.

To do this, we would register our own `SC.RecordAttribute` transform using `SC.RecordAttribute.registerTransform` to map between the raw value of the attribute and the complex object of the property.

For example:

```
SC.RecordAttribute.registerTransform(SC.Color, {
  /**
    Convert a String in the format 'rgb(###,###,###)' to an SC.Color.
  */
  to: function(stringValue, attr) {
    // If there is a value, convert it to an SC.Color.
    if (!SC.none(stringValue)) {
      stringValue = SC.Color.from(stringValue);
    }

    return stringValue;
  },

  /**
    Convert an SC.Color to a String in the format 'rgb(###,###,###)'
  */
```

```
    from: function(colorValue, attr) {
      // If there is a value, convert it to a String.
      if (!SC.none(colorValue)) {
        colorValue = colorValue.toRgb();
      }

      return colorValue;
    }
  });
```

Once you've added a custom transform type, you can use it in any of your records. The following is an example of a pen record that contains a color attribute using our previous transform:

```
MyApp.Pen = SC.Record.extend({

  color: SC.Record.attr(SC.Color)

});
```

Although you may not use this functionality right away, it's good to know that it exists and you may find it to be a nice way to clean up your code, if you find you need a lot of data transformations in your application.

Defining record relationships

This brings us to the last type of attribute we will use: the relationship attribute. Records are often related to each other as one-to-one, one-to-many, or many-to-many and we can encode this hierarchy in our SproutCore data model as well. To indicate a relationship, we use one of either SC.SingleAttribute (that is, to one) or SC.ManyAttribute (that is, to many), which is done just like we did with SC.RecordAttribute by using SC.Record helper methods. In this case, the helpers are toOne and toMany to be exact.

For example, if you recall from our simple data model example of Calendar and Event records, we indicated a relationship between the two. This relationship will exist in the raw data on the server, such that Calendar records will contain an array of Event record IDs and Event records will contain a single Calendar ID. To add this relationship to our classes, we would update the records as follows:

```
MyApp.Calendar = SC.Record.extend({

  // This calendar's events.
  events: SC.Record.toMany('MyApp.Event')

});
```

```
MyApp.Event = SC.Record.extend({

  // This event's calendar.
  calendar: SC.Record.toOne('MyApp.Calendar')

});
```

 Notice that the attributes are of string type (that is, `'MyApp.Event'`). We use strings so that we don't have to deal with the tricky problem of which record class is to be loaded first. When the attribute is used for the first time, the proper record class will actually be looked up.

Just like with the `attr` helper method, we can pass options to `toOne` and `toMany`. Since `SC.SingleAttribute` and `SC.ManyAttribute` inherit from `SC.RecordAttribute`, we can use the `isEditable` and `key` options just the same, but there are two other options specific to relationship attributes: `inverse` and `isMaster`.

The `inverse` option is the name of the property on the other side of the relationship, which, when set, will modify the other side of the relationship when this side changes. This sounds a bit tricky, but it's quite simple once you get it.

Let's look at what happens when we modify the relationship without the `inverse` option declared. To show this, I've mocked up a few sample records. There are two Calendar records with the guid **'calendar1'** and **'calendar2'** respectively and there are three Event records with the guid **'event1'**, **'event2'**, and **'event3'** respectively. For this demo, all of the three events originally belong to **'calendar1'**.

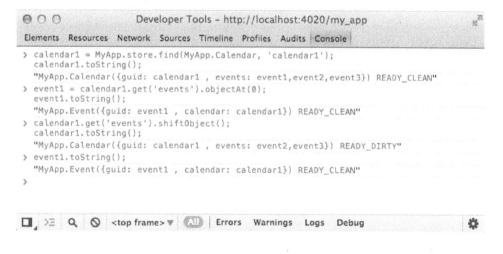

This simulation shows a couple of things we're not familiar with yet, but let me walk you through it. The basics of what I did are that I retrieved a calendar record as well as the first event related to that calendar. By using the **toString** method of each of these records, I was able to see that **calendar1**'s **events** attribute includes 'event1' and **event1**'s **calendar** attribute was 'calendar1'. But see what happened after I shifted the first record out of **calendar1**? While **calendar1** now showed two events correctly, **event1** still believed that it was related to **calendar1**. If we neglected to fix this up, we could have a serious data inconsistency problem later on.

The **READY_CLEAN** and **READY_DIRTY** strings in the **Console** example explain the status of the records. We will look at the life cycle and all the possible status of records in the next portion.

But do we need to manually fix up both sides of a relationship? Why don't we add inverse options to our models and try again.

First, I will add the inverse to each of the relationship as shown in the following code:

```
MyApp.Calendar = SC.Record.extend({

  // This calendar's events.
  events: SC.Record.toMany('MyApp.Event', {
    inverse: 'calendar'  // The attribute name on the other side of
the relationship.
  })

});

MyApp.Event = SC.Record.extend({

  // This event's calendar.
  calendar: SC.Record.toOne('MyApp.Calendar', {
    inverse: 'events'  // The attribute name on the other side of
the relationship.
  })

});
```

Next, I will run the mock example again in the console as shown in the following screenshot:

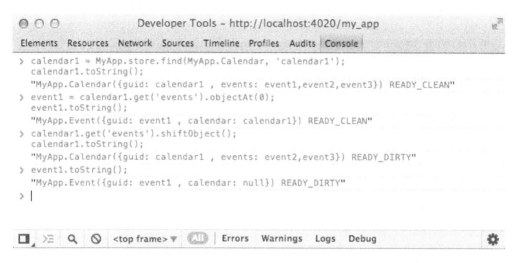

Wonderful! Now, when we inspect the **event1** record after altering the relationship on the calendar side, we see that its relationship has also been modified, which is exactly what we want. Please note that since we specified the inverse of calendar in **MyApp.Event** as well, the same rule would have applied had we changed **event1**'s **calendar** attribute instead of **calendar1**'s **events** attribute.

Now, we'll look at the `isMaster` option for relationship attributes. It's actually important to have a good understanding of the `inverse` option in hand because the `isMaster` option is directly related to it. To be clear, the first thing to remember is that `isMaster` is only used along with `inverse`. To describe what `isMaster` does, we have to skip ahead a bit and pay attention to how the status of the records changed from **READY_CLEAN** to **READY_DIRTY** when we modified the relationships in the previous examples.

All you need to know right now is that the **READY_CLEAN** state is the state of a record when it has no changes and the **READY_DIRTY** state is the state of a record that has changes. If a record is dirty, we expect to commit the changes back to a remote data source so that our data between the client and server is synchronized. However, it is likely that we only need to commit changes to one side of a relationship and the remote data source will understand that the other side has changed as well.

For example, if we moved **event1** from **calendar1** to **calendar2**, we would dirty three records, which could become three commits back to the server. But every API can recognize that if **event1** has changed its relationship with **calendar2**, it also has to update **calendar1** and **calendar2**. Therefore, we only need to dirty the Event record when the event to calendar relationship changes. This is what `isMaster` does for us in a record relationship. If we set `isMaster` to `false`, changes in the relationship will not dirty the record.

 The value of `isMaster` is `true` by default.

Here's an example to help make this clear. First, we indicate that Calendars are not the master of the relationship and need not be dirtied when the events relationship changes.

```
MyApp.Calendar = SC.Record.extend({

  events: SC.Record.toMany('MyApp.Event', {
    inverse: 'calendar',
    isMaster: false  // Changes to this relationship only dirty the
event record
  })

});
```

Next, we go back to the **Console** to see it in action:

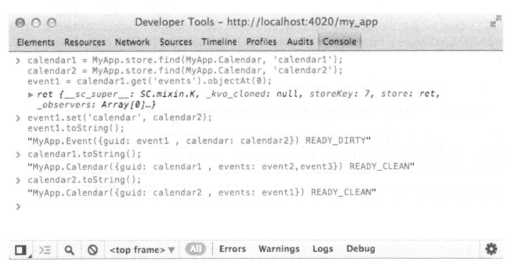

Can you spot the difference? This time once the relationship is altered, only the Event record is placed in a dirty state, which means only it will be committed back to the server.

Now, I realize that these examples have stepped well into the realm of the SC.Record life cycle and so, let's continue on that path and look at it all in the next section.

At some point, you will undoubtedly come across nested record relationships. These seem like the normal relationship attributes, but are actually quite different. Nested relationships transform embedded JavaScript objects in the data hash into SC.Record instances. This allows you to use the objects like any other SC.Object/SC.Record object, including binding to properties, adding computed properties, and so forth. However, up to Version 1.10, nested records have remained somewhat temperamental and it's best to avoid using them until such time that the code has been refactored. In the meantime, it is safer to stick to a normal JavaScript object as the attribute type.

Following the life cycle of SC.Record

Records in SproutCore follow a life cycle similar to records in any other database, but with an important difference. Since the SproutCore store hosts the data only temporarily (remember it's a quick access cache representing remote data), we don't actually perform final data modifications within the application. Instead, we invoke requests and modifications (Create, Read, Update, Destroy) on a remote data store and update our local record state to match them.

We've already seen that records have a status value, such as SC.Record.READY_ CLEAN, which indicates the current state of the record. To help us understand every possible state in the life cycle of a SproutCore record, I've created figures of the SC.Record states. You should find these figures useful when you begin working with records. We will refer back to them repeatedly in this section as we learn how to load, unload, create, read, update, and ultimately destroy records.

The following figure shows the static states of a record and the methods on the store that we use for transition between them. The methods are on the store because the store manages the state of each record and so, ultimately determines how the record state should change.

Note that transitions are not immediate and so, there are several intermediate busy states that exist while we wait for a confirmation from the remote data source. As you can see in the figure, the record will typically be in one of the six static states: READY_NEW, READY_CLEAN, READY_DIRTY, DESTROYED_DIRTY, DESTROYED_CLEAN, or EMPTY. We will look at each of these states in more detail shortly.

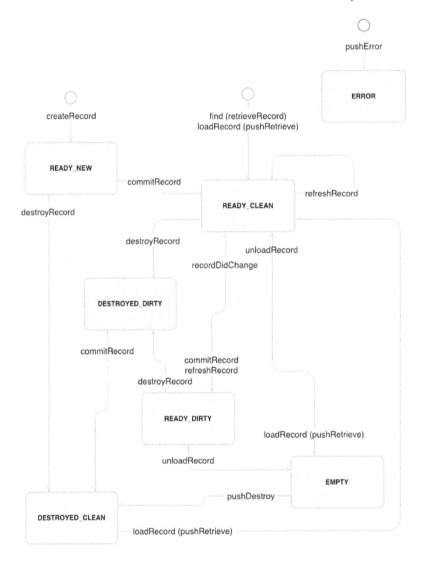

Loaded records (READY_CLEAN)

The SproutCore data store includes support for loading and unloading records. Loading a record is different from creating a record because the record has already been created somewhere on a remote store and we are just loading it temporarily for use within our application. Likewise, unloading a record is not the same as destroying one because the real remote record is not actually being destroyed.

To load a record, we call `loadRecord` on the store. This method takes the type of the record and the data hash of the record as arguments. You can also pass the ID as the third argument but in case you don't, it will be looked up from within the data hash according to the record's `primaryKey` value.

For example:

```
var storeKey;

storeKey = MyApp.store.loadRecord(MyApp.Calendar, {
  guid: 'calendar3',
  title: "Birthdays"
});
```

As you can see from the state figure, a record that is loaded will initially be in the READY_CLEAN state, which means it is synchronized with the remote data store as far as we know.

The return value for `loadRecord` is the unique `storeKey` value for the record. Store keys represent how the store manages its records internally. Because the same ID may be shared between different types of records and because newly created records usually have no ID, the store generates a unique store key to properly identify each record. We will find that we use the store key from time to time when working with the store, and you can retrieve it from the record if you need.

For example:

```
storeKey = myRecord.get('storeKey');
```

Finally, as we will see with each of these methods, there is a multiple record version of `loadRecord`, which is `loadRecords`. To use `loadRecords` or any of the other pluralized methods, we simply pass the same arguments, but within arrays.

You will notice in the figure that `loadRecord` appears each time with `pushRetrieve` in parenthesis. This is because the `loadRecord` method is really a wrapper over `pushRetrieve` and `dataSourceDidComplete` (a method we will look at later) and depending on the state of the record, calls the appropriate method.

Unloaded records (EMPTY)

In a lot of SproutCore applications, the number of records can exceed thousands, tens of thousands, and even millions of records. In such a scenario, it is absolutely necessary to also unload records in order to free the memory. To unload a record that has been loaded, we call `unloadRecord` on the store and pass either the record type and ID or the store key to it.

For example:

```
MyApp.store.unloadRecord(MyApp.Calendar, 'calendar3');
```

This is equivalent to the following code:

```
MyApp.store.unloadRecord(null, null, aCalendar.get('storeKey'));
```

 Note that once a record is unloaded, it still exists in the store but will be in the EMPTY state and have no data hash. Unloading multiple records is done with `unloadRecords`.

To be read records (BUSY_LOADING and BUSY_REFRESH)

This sub-section is titled "To be read records" rather than "Reading records" because we aren't doing the actual reading from the remote database directly. Due to this slight semantic difference, the record we receive from the store will either be in the BUSY_LOADING or one of the two BUSY_REFRESH states while it is actually being read from the remote source and sent to us. The following figure shows these additional busy states.

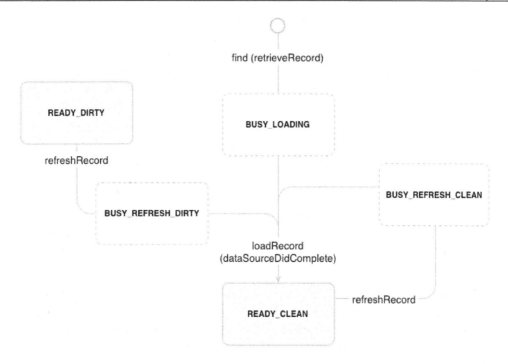

The typical way we request records is with the `find` method on the store. We can retrieve all records of a type by passing the record type to `find`. If we pass a specific ID as the second argument, it will return just the matching record of that type. We can also retrieve all records that match certain conditions by passing a query object to `find`.

For example:

```
// An SC.RecordArray of event records.
allEvents = MyApp.store.find(MyApp.Event);

// A single event record.
event = MyApp.store.find(MyApp.Event, 'event1');

// An SC.RecordArray of event records starting after now.
futureEvents = MyApp.store.find(SC.Query.create({
  recordType: MyApp.Event,
  conditions: "startAt > " + (new Date()).getTime()
});
```

The previous example introduces an important class in the SproutCore Model layer that we haven't looked at yet, `SC.RecordArray`. When we retrieve a group of records, the returned object is always a record array, which is like a normal array, but has a status value that we can use to know when the actual array was filled. Record arrays are also able to update their contents live from the store when they are based on local query objects. We'll look more at working with query objects later on in this chapter.

Another thing to know is that the `find` method is actually just a wrapper over `retrieveRecord`, `materializeRecord`, and some internal code for handling query objects. When you call `find` with a record type and ID, it will call `retrieveRecord` if the record isn't loaded, in order to retrieve it from the remote source or will call `materializeRecord` if it is loaded, to return an instance of the record class. While you will likely never use `retrieveRecord` over `find`, the plural version `retrieveRecords` allows you to request a specific set of record IDs at once, which may be of use.

Lastly, the other store method shown in the figure is the `refreshRecord` method. We can call this on already loaded records in order to re-fetch their data from the remote source. Depending on the current state of the loaded record, this will put the record into the `BUSY_REFRESH_CLEAN` or `BUSY_REFRESH_DIRTY` state.

To be created records (READY_NEW)

Creating a new record in the client is simple enough. We simply call `createRecord` on the store and pass the type of record, the data hash for the record, and optionally an ID for the record. Typically, you will not have an ID for the record yet because assigning unique IDs is usually the job of the remote data store.

For example:

```
newCalendar = MyApp.store.createRecord(MyApp.Calendar, { title:
"Family" });

console.log(newCalendar.toString());
// > MyApp.Calendar({title: Family}) READY_NEW
```

As you can see from the static record states figure, a call to `createRecord` is the only entry point to the `READY_NEW` state. This state indicates that the record can be used but has not yet been created in the remote data store.

Use `createRecords` to create multiple records at once.

 Remember that we use attribute names and not property names in the data hash. For instance, if the `displayPrice` property uses the `display_price` key, the data hash passed to `createRecord` should contain a `display_price` attribute.

To be updated records (READY_DIRTY)

Once a record is in the `READY_CLEAN` state, modifications to its attributes will automatically move it to the `READY_DIRTY` state. The dirty state indicates that the record is no longer synchronized with the remote data store and that the remote data store will need to be updated.

In the static record state figure, the connection between `READY_CLEAN` and `READY_DIRTY` shows the `recordDidChange` method of the store. While you could call this, you won't typically need to, since it will be called for us by using key-value coding (that is, `set`) to change the record attributes.

There is also a `recordsDidChange` method for indicating multiple record changes.

To be destroyed records (DESTROYED_DIRTY)

Destroying a record on the client is again very simple. The store provides the `destroyRecord` and `destroyRecords` methods that work almost identically to the `unloadRecord` and `unloadRecords` methods. This means that you pass the same arguments to `destroyRecord`, either the record type and ID or the store key of the record. The difference is that with `destroyRecord`, the data hash of the record is not immediately cleared and its state becomes `DESTROYED_DIRTY`, indicating that it needs to be synchronized with the server.

For example:

```
MyApp.store.destroyRecord(MyApp.Calendar, toBeDestroyedCalendar.
get('id'));

console.log(toBeDestroyedCalendar.toString());
// > MyApp.Calendar({guid: work-calendar, title: Work}) DESTROYED_
DIRTY
```

By the way, we can get the same result by simply calling destroy on the record instance as shown in the following code line:

```
toBeDestroyedCalendar.destroy();
```

We will look at how to complete the transition between the DESTROYED_DIRTY and DESTROYED_CLEAN states shortly.

Querying the store

Before we look at synchronizing data with a remote source, we do have to catch up on how to use the queries that we briefly saw when we introduced find. Firstly, there are two types of queries: local and remote. I'll warn you now not to get hung up on the names; using both types of queries may invoke a fetch to a remote data source. The difference is that the content and order of local queries is updated live depending on the current records in the local store, while the content and order of remote queries is set by the remote data source and can only be updated by requesting from the remote data source again.

Why have this distinction? It's simple. If you have 5,000,000 records on your server, you don't want to load them all into your application in order to perform a search for just 10 of them. Therefore, *when the results of the query depend on a set of data too large to be loaded entirely into the client store, we use remote queries*. When the query is based on what is loaded in the store, we can use local queries. For example, we always load the data most relevant to what the user is doing in the client. If the user then wants to do a search, we could use a local query to search the few hundred records that we've loaded extremely quickly, in order to present some best effort results immediately to the user. If the user wants to do an expanded search, we would run a remote query to get additional search results from the server.

To create a query, we create an instance of SC.Query as shown in the following code snippet:

```
query = SC.Query.create({
  recordType: 'MyApp.Event'
});
```

The query type is determined by the value of the location property, which is SC.Query.LOCAL by default. So, the previous code snippet would create a local query for records of type MyApp.Event with no conditions. This will, in turn, return all the event records in the store, which to drive the point home, may not be all the event records in existence, since there may still be tens of thousands of more records on the server that have not yet been loaded in the application.

Let's look at creating a remote query first. A lot of remote queries are unique and don't change. So, we can create them once for use across the entire application. It's important to reuse rather than recreate identical queries because the store can then track which queries it has filled and not re-fetch a query that has already been filled, unless explicitly requested. If instead, we create a new query instance, even if it looks to be the same as one that has been filled already, the store will try to fill the new query with another round trip request to the server.

To create a remote query, we generally use the `SC.Query.remote helper` method. For example, these two approaches yield the same result:

```
// Example 1: using SC.Query.create
MyApp.peopleQuery = SC.Query.create({
  location: SC.Query.REMOTE,
  recordType: MyApp.Person,
  // Information to pass to the data source adaptor.
  includeAddress: true
});

// Example 2: using SC.Query.remote helper
MyApp.peopleQuery = SC.Query.remote(MyApp.Person, { includeAddress:
true });
```

Using the previous code, we can now call `MyApp.store.find(MyApp.peopleQuery)` anywhere in the application to get a record array of people records filtered and ordered by the server. By the way, did you notice the two ways we attached the `includeAddress` property to the query? The data source adaptor handling this query will use this property to determine which kind of request it should make. We'll see this again later.

Let's look at local queries now. These are more interesting than remote queries and great for providing that extremely fast user experience we're after. We've already seen how to create a local query instance using `create` but of course, there is a helper method too: `SC.Query.local`.

For example:

```
MyApp.peopleQuery = SC.Query.local(MyApp.Person);
```

However, when we query for the records locally, we usually want to filter and order the results. First, to order the results, we can set the orderBy property. The simplest way to order results is by using an order string like it is commonly found in SQL languages. For example, to order by firstName and lastName, we use the following code snippet:

```
MyApp.peopleQuery = SC.Query.local(MyApp.Person, {
  orderBy: 'firstName, lastName DESC'
});
```

The default order is ascending or ASC. So, the query in this example will order people by firstName in ascending order first and then by lastName in descending order. The orderBy property can also be set to a standard comparison function for more advanced comparisons.

Next, to filter the records according to specific criteria, we can set conditions on the query. SC.Query includes an incredible SQL-like query language called the **SproutCore Query Language (SCQL)**.

SCQL allows us to make conditional queries such as shown in the following code snippet:

```
// All people that are minors.
MyApp.minorsQuery = SC.Query.local(MyApp.Person, {
  conditions: 'age < 21'
});
Or:
// All items for sale with names beginning with searchName.
MyApp.localSearchQuery = SC.Query.local(MyApp.Item, {
  conditions: '(name BEGINS_WITH "' + searchName + '") AND (isForSale
= true)'
});
```

There are several other operators that you can construct conditions with, such as !=, ENDS_WITH, CONTAINS, MATCHES, and NOT, but I will leave it up to you to look these up in the documentation for SC.Query.

Also, as you must have probably noticed by now, inserting dynamic parameters into the conditions string like we did with searchName in the previous example is not very nice. An improvement would be to mark the parameters in the conditions string and pass them as variables, which is exactly what we can do.

For example, the previous example is better written in the following way:

```
var searchName = 'Ro';

// All items for sale with names beginning with 'searchLetter'.
MyApp.localSearchQuery = SC.Query.local(MyApp.Item, {
  conditions: '(name BEGINS_WITH "{name}") AND (isForSale = true)',
  parameters: { name: searchName }
});
```

As you can see, the name value will be looked up in the parameters object and inserted into the conditions string where we specified it. If you're creating complex local queries, you will no doubt find this to be a cleaner approach.

Finally, queries can also be re-fetched after they have been filled using the refreshQuery method on the store or simply by calling refresh on the query's associated record array.

For example:

```
// Run a query on the store (the first time will go to the server).
var results = MyApp.store.find(MyApp.localSearchQuery);

// Later… Refresh the query (will go to the server again).
results.refresh();
```

Synchronizing data with a remote data source

Finally, there is the matter of invoking the real **Create-Read-Update-Destroy (CRUD)** actions on the data, which will ultimately be performed in a remote data store. We have already seen the busy states while reading data, so let's look at the additional busy states while creating, updating, and destroying data.

As we can see from the previous figure, all three of these processes are started using the `commitRecord` method of the store. As we've seen before, when calling `commitRecord`, we pass in either the record type and ID or the store key. But we can pass a parameter's object too, which can be used to pass information to the data source adaptor about how the commit should be handled.

For example:

```
MyApp.store.destroyRecord(MyApp.Calendar, aCalendar.get('id'));

// Commit the change and pass online/offline information through to
the adaptor
MyApp.store.commitRecord(MyApp.Calendar, aCalendar.get('id'), null, {
  // We will target different remote stores depending on if we are
online or not.
  target: SC.device.get('isOffline') ? 'offlineDataStore' :
'liveDataStore'
});

console.log(aCalendar.toString());
// > MyApp.Calendar({guid: work-calendar, title: Work}) BUSY_
DESTROYING
```

We can commit each record individually as you've come to expect the presence of the `commitRecords` method for committing multiple records at once. However, what is important to know is that if we don't need to pass any arguments to `commitRecords`, it will instead, commit all the records in the store that are in an unsynchronized state (that is, READY_NEW, READY_DIRTY, or DESTROYED_DIRTY).

> You can also set `commitRecordsAutomatically` to
> `true` on the store and as a result, `commitRecords` will
> be called automatically each time we use `createRecord`,
> `recordDidChange`, or `destroyRecord`.

This brings us to the question of what happens after we commit records. As we touched upon this when we first introduced the SproutCore data store, the store is meant to work with a remote data adaptor, which transforms serialized data from a remote data source into data hashes for the store to use and vice versa. Therefore, calling `commitRecords` causes the store to ask its data source adaptor to actually perform the synchronization by communicating with the remote data source.

There is an amendment to this. We can actually chain stores together in order to queue up a number of changes inside a chained or nested store that is separate from the main store. In this way, we can modify a record temporarily without affecting the rest of the application. If we decide to throw the edits away, we can simply discard all the changes in the nested store and nothing will be changed in the main store. But if we want to keep the changes, we can commit them back up to the next store in the chain. Only when the changes are *committed back to the root store* will they actually be synchronized using a remote data source.

Implementing remote data source adaptors

The data source adaptor API is fairly simple, but can be difficult to use if you aren't told that the data sources act independently of the rest of the application and only the store interacts with them. This means that our application doesn't really know what the data source is doing, which is fine because the application need only be concerned with those records that it is using and their current status.

Because each data source is unique to its remote counterpart, we can't work through every possible scenario. Instead, we'll look at writing a fairly standard JSON adaptor which you can modify to match your particular backend as needed.

To create a data source, we extend SC.DataSource and typically place the file in a directory called data_sources.

For example, if we wanted to create a main data source, we would place the code in the app directory under datasources/main_data_source.js:

```
// @singleton - Data source for MyApp.
MyApp.mainDataSource = SC.DataSource.create({
  // ...
});
```

To assign the data source to the store, we can use the from helper method:

```
// MyApp.
MyApp = SC.Application.create({

  store: SC.Store.create().from('MyApp.mainDataSource'),

});
```

This is equivalent to writing the following code snippet:

```
store: SC.Store.create({
  dataSource: 'MyApp.mainDataSource'
}),
```

 We use a string to set the dataSource property so that we don't have to worry about the load order of the code. The real data source object will be looked up the first time it is needed.

Reading records

At this point, we are ready to actually request records on behalf of the store. Reading records is the most complicated feature to explain, so we'll do that first. The reason it is the most complicated is because there are three different types of reads that we can support. The first type is a fetch, which occurs the first time you try to find a query on the store. To fill queries, the store will call fetch on its data source, passing in itself and the query as arguments. All the data source needs to do is determine how to fill the query according to the remote data source it is working with, and then tell the store when it is done.

The following code is an example of filling both a local and a remote query for MyApp.Person records. In this example, the data source looks at the query type in order to determine which resource from the server will best fill its needs.

```
/** Triggered by MyApp.store.find(query) */
fetch: function (store, query) {
  var handled = true,
    recordType = query.recordType,
    request,
    url;

  // Fetching person records will be our queue to load resources
from the server.
  if (recordType === MyApp.Person) {
    if (query.get('isLocal')) {

      // Local (i.e. client ordered results)
      url = '/friends';
    } else {
```

```
      // Remote (i.e. server ordered results)
      url = '/top_ten';
    }

    // Send the request.
    request = SC.Request.getUrl(url)
      .json()
      .notify(this, '_didFetch', {
        query: query,
        store: store
      })
      .send();
  } else {

    // This query wasn't handled by the data source.
    handled = false;
  }

  return handled;
},

/** @private Callback for JSON fetch requests. */
_didFetch: function (response, params) {
  if (SC.ok(response)) {
    var body = response.get('body'),
      query = params.query,
      store = params.store,
      storeKeys;

    // Load the new records into the store.
    storeKeys = store.loadRecords(MyApp.Person, body.people);

    // Indicate that the query has been filled (storeKeys will be
ignored for local queries).
    store.dataSourceDidFetchQuery(query, storeKeys);
  }
```

To indicate that a query has been filled, we call dataSourceDidFetchQuery on
the store. For a remote query, we must pass the ordered array of store keys for the
results as well. Note that before the call to dataSourceDidFetchQuery, the record
array for the query will be in the BUSY_LOADING state, and will move to the READY_
CLEAN state afterwards. Also note that the data source returns true only if it handles
the request.

The next type of read is for retrieving a single record which occurs when we attempt to find a record by ID that doesn't exist in the store. Again, the store will ask its data source to fill the request for the record, this time by calling `retrieveRecord` on the data source. This type of request is even simpler to implement in the data source. All we need to do is call `loadRecord` with the data we receive.

For example:

```
/** Triggered by MyApp.store.find(RecordClass, id) */
retrieveRecord: function (store, storeKey, id) {
  var handled = true,
    recordType = store.recordTypeFor(storeKey),
    request;

  if (recordType === MyApp.Item) {
    // Send the request.
    request = SC.Request.getUrl('/items/' + id)
      .json()
      .notify(this, '_didRetrieve', {
        store: store,
        recordType: recordType
      })
      .send();
  } else {

    // This retrieve wasn't handled by the data source.
    handled = false;
  }

  return handled;
},

/** @private Callback for JSON retrieve requests. */
_didRetrieve: function (response, params) {
  if (SC.ok(response)) {
    var store = params.store,
      recordType = params.recordType,
      body = response.get('body');

    store.loadRecord(recordType, body);
  }
}
```

Finally, there is the third type of read, which is to retrieve multiple records by ID at once by implementing `retrieveRecords` in the data source. This is different from the others because this type of read is triggered by passing a set of specific record IDs to the store's `retrieveRecords` method. However, it is rare to find an API that allows you to retrieve multiple records by ID in a single request. In any case, you would handle it in the data source exactly the same way you handle `retrieveRecord`, just by substituting multiple IDs in place of the single ID.

Creating, updating, and destroying records

Now that we've seen how to implement reading, you will find that the other methods are simpler and very similar, whether we're creating, updating, or destroying the records. The only usual difference between them is that the actual request method made is different (for example, POST vs. GET), and that we don't need to call `loadRecord` when destroying records.

The following code is an example data source support for creating and editing records with a JSON backend:

```
/** Triggered by readyNewRecord.commitRecord() */
createRecord: function (store, storeKey, params) {
  var handled = true,
    recordType = store.recordTypeFor(storeKey),
    request;

  if (recordType === MyApp.Item) {
    // Send the request.
    request = SC.Request.postUrl('/items)
      .json()
      .notify(this, '_didCreateOrUpdate', {
        store: store,
        recordType: recordType
      })
      .send();
  } else {

    // This create wasn't handled by the data source.
    handled = false;
  }

  return handled;
},
```

```
/** Triggered by readyDirtyRecord.commitRecord() */
updateRecord: function (store, storeKey, params) {
  var handled = true,
    id = store.idFor(storeKey),
    recordType = store.recordTypeFor(storeKey),
    request;

  if (recordType === MyApp.Item) {
    // Send the request.
    request = SC.Request.putUrl('/items/' + id)
      .json()
      .notify(this, '_didCreateOrUpdate', {
        store: store,
        recordType: recordType
      })
      .send();
  } else {

    // This update wasn't handled by the data source.
    handled = false;
  }

  return handled;
},

/** @private Callback for JSON create and update requests. */
_didCreateOrUpdate: function (response, params) {
  if (SC.ok(response)) {
    var store = params.store,
      recordType = params.recordType,
      body = response.get('body');

    store.loadRecord(recordType, body);
  }
}
```

In this particular example, because creating and updating are so similar, we can in fact use the same callback function for the request. Again, this will all depend on the particular backend you are working with.

Finally, the last method to implement on the data source is `destroyRecord`, which we would do in a very similar fashion.

For example:

```
/** Triggered by destroyedDirtyRecord.commitRecord() */
destroyRecord: function (store, storeKey, params) {
  var handled = true,
    id = store.idFor(storeKey),
    recordType = store.recordTypeFor(storeKey),
    request;
  if (recordType === MyApp.Item) {
    // Send the request.
    request = SC.Request.deleteUrl('/items/' + id)
      .json()
      .notify(this, '_didDestroy', {
        store: store,
        storeKey: storeKey
      })
      .send();
  } else {

    // This destroy wasn't handled by the data source.
    handled = false;
  }

  return handled;
},

/** @private Callback for JSON destroy requests. */
_didDestroy: function (response, params) {
  if (SC.ok(response)) {
    var store = params.store,
      storeKey = params.recordType;

    // Indicate that the record has indeed been destroyed.
    store.dataSourceDidDestroy(storeKey);
  }
}
```

 There are methods that can be used to modify several records with a single request if the remote data source supports it. These methods are `createRecords`, `updateRecords`, and `destroyRecords`.

With these examples, it actually takes care of all the fundamentals of creating a data source. Just remember that the actual request and response handling code in your application is specific to the remote data source that you are working with and so, you may find that your actual data source code looks quite different to these examples. But still, you will use the same store callbacks in the same manner: `dataSourceDidFetchQuery`, `loadRecord`, `loadRecords`, and `dataSourceDidDestroy`.

The only other thing I need to do is remind you of the fixtures data source, `SC.FixturesDataSource`, that we saw in *Chapter 1, Introducing SproutCore*. Fixtures are essential when the remote source isn't quite ready for use. But even if the remote source is usable, developing against fixture data is much faster and provides you with a well-known environment to work in.

Summary

So, this was a long chapter but for good reasons because there is a lot of functionality in the Model layer to cover. So far we've looked at what the Model layer and Data Interface layers are in a SproutCore application, at SproutCore's client-side data store, at modeling data in the application, and at modeling relationships in the application. We also studied the entire life cycle of a SproutCore record and looked at how to query local and remote data stores. Lastly, we looked at how we would write our own data source adaptors to synchronize local records with a remote store.

At this point, you should be able to define an entire data model for your own applications and use a SproutCore data store to retrieve and modify the data locally. You should also be able to recognize the difference between local and remote queries and know how to run queries against local or remote stores. Most importantly, you should completely understand the life cycle of a SproutCore record including the methods you use to move the record from one state to another.

Don't be alarmed if it seems like a lot to digest all at once. When you begin working on your own application, you can come back to this chapter as and when needed, to review the fundamentals.

In the next chapter, we will tie it all together by connecting our models to our views and adding the logic that will really turn our application into software.

5
The Controller Layer

In this chapter we will look at the C in SproutCore MVC or the Controller layer. As it turns out, the role of the Controller layer in SproutCore is as a proxy, and since SproutCore does so much of it automatically for us, we don't actually need a full chapter to discuss it. But just as we have discussed the Display layer alongside the View layer and the Data Interface layer alongside the Model layer, we will spend most of this chapter looking at the close companion to the Controller layer, the Application State layer.

Although the term Application State is something that I have coined for this book, it's not that the term is based on a new idea. In reality, the application state exists within all software applications, but is generally not identified as it is mixed within the other MVC or similarly themed layers. For example, in early SproutCore, developers put most of what we will discover as the Application State layer inside the Controller layer.

However, that is no longer the case and we will see how separating out the controller functions from the application state functions provides us with a powerful new approach to improving code structure, safety, and overall quality. As a part of this, we will introduce the concept of statecharts and learn how we can use SproutCore's statechart library to turn that theory into functioning code.

In this chapter we will cover the following:

- Understanding the Controller and Application State layers
- Working with SproutCore's controllers
- Designing with statecharts
- Avoiding pitfalls with statecharts
- Coding with statecharts

Understanding the Controller and Application State layers

As I have mentioned in the opening paragraph, the Controller layer is actually a minor layer in SproutCore. This wasn't always the case; but with the addition of the statechart library to SproutCore, it became obvious that the best way to structure a SproutCore application, and likely any application, is by using statechart theory. Let me take a moment to make myself clear.

It's safe to say that every single application has (what we can call) a state. As soon as an application starts running, it will enter at least one state and likely enter and exit several other states before completion. This may include states of loading data, awaiting input, editing a record, saving to a database, being offline, or any other number of context specific states.

But while we, the developers, can easily recognize these states, this recognition doesn't always translate into the code. Unfortunately, very few frameworks provide tools to the code application states properly, and as it turns out, the inability to maintain state is the source of almost all programming problems. I'm sure this is a bold statement to make, but one that I believe plays itself out time and time again as other apps crash, freeze, or get exploited by hackers. For now, it's enough for us to agree that when an application is in a certain state, no matter how that state is defined, it should only be able to do certain actions and go to certain other states. This is like saying, when we are in an editing state, we should only be able to perform actions such as save changes and discard changes.

Of course, developers recognize this and do a number of things to try and maintain the overall application state. A common approach is to set flags such as `isSaving` or `isReady` that other pieces of code are expected to use in order to gate keep the appropriate code paths. Now I'm generally very open to alternative coding patterns, but I have seen flag setting fail so many times that I'm going to write emphatically, this does not work!

There are two huge problems with using flags to maintain application state. The first is that because the state is a combination of flags spread across the entire application, the actual real state is never very clear. But worse than this is that when flags change in multiple spots, we invariably introduce the most dreaded of all bugs, the race condition. These are the bugs that suddenly appear in production, but aren't reproducible in development or that affect one user and not the other, because they occur from seemingly negligible time differences to the order of when flags toggle that allows the application to enter invalid states that the developer had never considered.

But, enough about the wrong way to go about it; instead, we shall formalize the Application State layer separate from the other MVC layers. The Application State layer will be in charge of maintaining the real application state and will handle all of the actions and events that may alter the state of the application. Because this layer understands the overall application state, it can also coordinate and configure MVC layers as the state changes that gives us additional opportunities to fine-tune the performance of our application by doing things such as lazily adding bindings and observers or loading code through modules (more about this is in *Chapter 6, Testing, Building, and Deploying*).

Finally, with the state of the application no longer the responsibility of the controller layer, where does that leave the controller layer? It's simple; the Controller layer simply mediates between the View and Model layers. In the next section, we'll look at how this works.

Working with SproutCore's controllers

Just as most of the objects in the View layer are views, we call the primary objects in the Controller layer as controllers. The base class for these controllers is the `SC.Controller` class, but it does essentially nothing more than the `SC.Object` class it extends, so we will always use one of its subclasses such as `SC.ObjectController`, `SC.ArrayController` or `SC.TreeController`. The role of these three types of controllers should be fairly self-evident. The `SC.ObjectController` subclass proxies a single object, `SC.ArrayController` proxies an array or array-like object and `SC.TreeController` proxies a tree-like object.

To use any of these controllers is a matter of creating the controller and setting its content property to the appropriate type of object. Once the content of the controller is set, we can use the controller as a proxy to the original object. In this way, the controller can translate between mismatched endpoints if necessary. Let's look at a couple of simple examples.

First, if we had a `MyApp.Person` model such as the following code:

```
MyApp.Person = SC.Record.extend({

    firstName: SC.Record.attr(String),

    lastName: SC.Record.attr(String)

});
```

we could create an object controller that would back a person's record shown as follows:

```
// Our person controller singleton.
MyApp.personController = SC.ObjectController.create();
```

The best part of this is that it gives us a single controller that the entire application can use to access the current person's record. Each time that we retrieve a person's record from the store and wish to display or edit it, we would set it as the content of this controller and anything bound to `MyApp.personController.content` would update accordingly. This same concept applies for the array and tree controllers as well.

We have already seen a few controller examples in *Chapter 1, Introducing SproutCore*, but before we move on, we should look at one more example to help clarify what mediating between the Model and View layers really means.

Using the preceding example code, let's play with our controller in the browser console. To prepare this, I will first push a sample `MyApp.Person` record to the store that we can use. Have a look at the following screenshot:

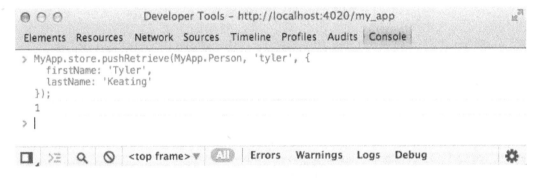

Now we can re-enact the simple pattern that I have described earlier, that is, to retrieve an object and set it as the content of a controller. For example, have a look at the following screenshot:

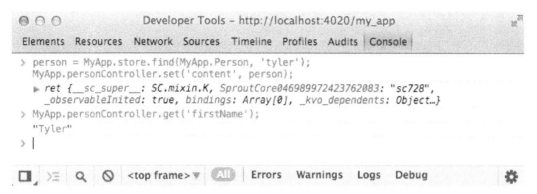

As you can see, once I've set the content of the controller, I can access the properties of the content directly on the controller. The way this works is that if the property doesn't exist on the controller itself, the controller will attempt to retrieve it from its content. This is the behavior we employ to provide more appropriate properties for use elsewhere in the app.

For example, in *Chapter 1, Introducing SproutCore,* we had a similar model to our `MyApp.Person` model called `Contacts.Contact`. If you recall, that model had a computed property, `fullName` that generated the full name of the contact. While having the model, providing the full name is not a bad idea; if you think about it, the full name of the person is actually a display property. For an instance, depending on the language or the user preference, full name may be `firstName lastName` or it may be `lastName firstName` or something slightly different. Does it make sense for the model to be connected directly to a global display property determining the name order? No, it doesn't. It would actually cause us a lot of trouble if we had to update all our records each time the user changed the way they wanted the full name to be displayed.

Instead, this is a place where our mediating controller can step in to provide a suitable property without modifying the underlying data layer to do so. Here's an updated `personController` that makes a proper `fullName` property available to any view or any other that wants it:

```
MyApp.personController = SC.ObjectController.create({
  /** Determine the display order of the full name. */
  displayOrder: 'lastName',

  fullName: function () {
    var displayOrder = this.get('displayOrder'),
```

```
        firstName = this.get('firstName'),
        lastName = this.get('lastName');

    if (displayOrder === 'lastName') {
      return [lastName + ',', firstName].compact().join(' ');
    } else {
      return [firstName, lastName].compact().join(' ');
    }
  }.property('firstName', 'lastName', 'displayOrder').cacheable()

});
```

And, here's our new controller in action once more:

See how easily we can modify the display order using the global person controller. You can imagine how having several views bound to the `fullName` property would allow you to toggle the `displayOrder` value to magically update all the views.

Be careful when setting or binding properties on an object controller. Just as `get` goes to the controller's content object, if the property doesn't exist on the controller, `set` will also set the value directly on the content object if the property isn't defined on the controller. To avoid accidentally dirtying the content object with a property meant only for the controller, be sure to always define the property on the controller.

SC.ArrayController

This controller is used to house a collection of objects such as an array or a set and is a very important and widely used controller in most SproutCore apps. The reason SC.ArrayController is so useful is because it not only proxies a collection of objects, but also automatically observes the collection for membership changes. This allows us to easily bind to arrays and other enumerables, simply by setting them as the content of an array controller and binding to that array controller.

Let's have a look at a basic array controller setup. We begin with a collection of items such as those returned by a query on the store.

```
var people = MyApp.store.find(MyApp.Person);
```

Which we simply assign as the content of a controller shown as follows:

```
MyApp.peopleController = SC.ArrayController.create({
  content: people
});
```

Once we've assigned the content, we can use the array controller much like any other enumerable. For example, have a look at the following screenshot:

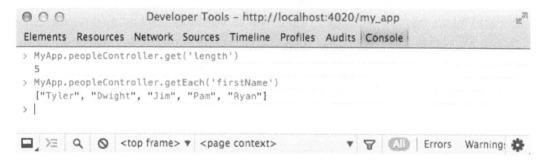

But, what we typically want to do with the controller is to bind it to a collection view so that we can display the items and have that display update automatically when the items change. For instance, this is exactly what we did in the *Connecting it all together* section from *Chapter 1, Introducing SproutCore*.

Here's some code from that tutorial that bound the content of an SC.ListView to the arrangedObjects property of an array controller:

```
contentView: SC.ListView.design({
    // The content for this list is contained in
  Contacts.groupsController.
    contentBinding: 'Contacts.groupsController.arrangedObjects'
```

The key thing to remember is that we should always access the array controller's content via the special `arrangedObjects` property. This is because we want to get the proxied version of the content, not the content itself, in case the array controller has transformed the content somehow.

Here's an example that shows this better and introduces one more special property of `SC.ArrayController` that we can use to order the content, called `orderBy`. In the first screenshot, we see that `arrangedObjects` and `content` appear to be the same.

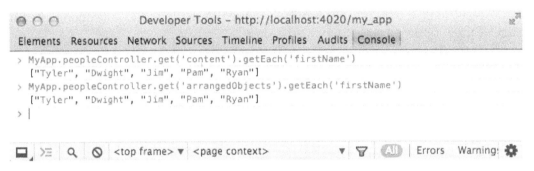

However, once we set an `orderBy` value, the original content and the content returned by `arrangedObjects` are different. This is because the controller is doing a simple sort transform on the content without actually modifying the original content.

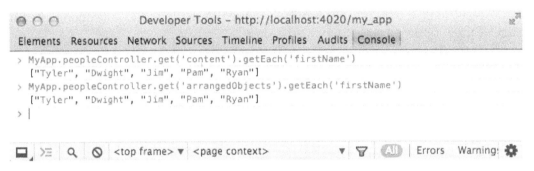

In this manner, the array controller can be used to provide data that is modified to meet the needs of whichever views are consuming it, including returning placeholder data for an empty array.

SC.TreeController

The final controller in SproutCore is used for managing tree-structured collections. Although `SC.TreeController` is not nearly as simple to use as `SC.ObjectController` or `SC.ArrayController`, because of its extreme power, you will definitely want to use a tree controller for any hierarchical data. Attempting to manage tree data on your own any other way would be a difficult and time-consuming task. What `SC.TreeController` does for us is that it provides an `arrangedObjects` property like `SC.ArrayController`, so that we can bind and display tree data in a collection view. Most importantly, it observes the tree structure for changes and automatically updates `arrangedObjects` as well.

The key to understanding tree controllers is really just to understand which properties must exist in the content to make the entire tree work. Once you know what the controller is looking for, it becomes much easier to use it without having to worry about the magic it's doing behind the scenes to transform your tree into displayable data.

Essentially, there are only two properties required by the controller: `treeItemChildren` and `treeItemIsExpanded`. By default, each object in the tree will be inspected for these two properties, which the controller will then use and observe for changes. If `treeItemChildren` of an object returns an array of other objects, that parent object will become a branch in the tree and if `treeItemChildren` returns `null`, that object will become a leaf in the tree.

To best include these properties to your model objects, we will mix in `SC.TreeItemContent` to the class, which defines these properties as well as some additional methods used by the controller and any list views displaying the content. For example, to be able to display an employee hierarchy, we would first mix in `SC.TreeItemContent` into the `MyApp.Employee` model. Have a look at the following code:

```
MyApp.Employee = SC.Record.extend(SC.TreeItemContent, {

    employees: SC.Record.toMany('MyApp.Employee'),

    name: SC.Record.attr(String)

});
```

We'll leave the value of `treeItemIsExpanded` as its default of `true`, so all we still need to do is provide the `treeItemChildren`, which in this case is the value of `employees`. One option would be to rename the `employees` attribute to `treeItemChildren`, but we may want to work with `employees` in different contexts and may not want to have its name be so ambiguous, so instead we should simply add a computed property for `treeItemChildren`. Have a look at the following code:

```
// ...

    treeItemChildren: function () {
      var employees = this.get('employees');

      // Return null so this employee is a leaf in the tree.
      if (SC.empty(employees)) { return null; }
      else { return employees; }
    }.property('employees')

// ...
```

We could also use different property names for `treeItemChildren` and `treeItemIsExpanded` by setting the values of `treeItemChildrenKey` and `treeItemIsExpandedKey` on the controller to some other names. However, as of Version 1.10, `SC.TreeItemContent` only respects using `treeItemChildren` and `treeItemIsExpanded`, so it's better if we use these property names.

Finally, we simply need to set the root object as the content of a tree controller so that we can start using it. For example, the root of the employee tree could be the president or CEO record.

```
// Create a tree controller to back the employees display.
MyApp.employeesTreeController = SC.TreeController.create();

// Retrieve the CEO record in some manner.
var ceo = MyApp.store.find(MyApp.Employee, 1);

// Assign the CEO as root of the tree controller.
MyApp.employeesTreeController.set('content', ceo);
```

Once our controller is set up, we use it like any other array controller and can bind its `arrangedObjects` property to a list view. There are some additional nuances to using tree controllers, but this should be enough to get you started. As well, all of these controllers appear in a number of SproutCore demos and so you can refer to the source code of the demos at `http://showcase.sproutcore.com` for more examples when you're ready.

> The root object of the tree controller does not appear in arrangedObjects. Therefore, if we wanted to include the CEO from the previous example in the list, we would simply create a wrapper root object like,
>
> ```
> rootObject = SC.Object.create(SC.TreeItemContent, {
>     treeItemChildren: [ceo]
> });
> ```

So there you have it, working with the array controller and tree controller is very similar to object controller, only using their respective content types and all in all it's pretty simple. However, that's not to gloss over the subtlety of using controllers with views and models appropriately. Good SproutCore development often doesn't mean writing a lot of code. Instead it means writing very little code, but only the right code. Knowing what code to write and where to put it takes some experience, but by this point you are well on your way. In fact, there is only one more major area to cover before we wrap up.

Designing with statecharts

Now, there are entire books written about statechart theory and so we won't even attempt to cover the entire topic in this small section, but that's fine. Like with most software development concepts, we can begin to apply the theory without having to know it all upfront. For our needs, we just need to recognize and remember the proper patterns and let time and practice make the theory clear to us.

Statecharts is a graphical language developed by professor David Harel that has been gaining popularity steadily due to its usefulness in modeling reactive systems. Using a statechart, we can design our application as a series of finite states that will respond (or not respond as it may be) to the many events and actions that occur. In this way, every possible function of our application can be described before being translated directly into code.

It's probably best to begin with an example diagram. The following is a simple statechart one might start with for an application:

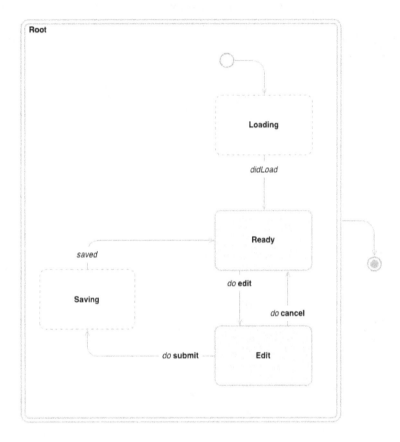

This application has five states: **Loading, Ready, Edit,** and **Saving** that are all substates of the **Root** state. In a statechart there is always one root state that has no parent.

While all of these states are technically equivalent, I've drawn the Loading and Saving states using a dashed line to reflect that these are transition states, which simply means that the application won't accept any user input while in these states. I've also drawn the Root state using a double line, to reflect that it has substates. If I had outlined any of the other states with a double line, you would know that state has substates within it, which, in order to keep the diagram easy-to-read, would be shown in a further diagram. There are also two special non-states, which I've drawn with circles. At the top of the diagram is the default entry point to the Root state, which is shown as an open circle and to the rightmost there is the end point for the entire statechart, which is shown as a circle within a circle.

Finally, there are the most important components to the diagram, the state transition arrows. These arrows tell us exactly how our application will change state and to which state it will change. To differentiate between events (things that happen) and actions (things that the user triggers), I've drawn the events in italics and the actions in bold. Having our state transition arrows properly defined gives us the entire picture of how our application will behave. For instance, while in the Loading state only the `didLoad` event will transition to the Ready state. From there if the user invokes the edit action, the application will transition to the Edit state, where the user may invoke either submit or cancel. As well, at any state inside the entire Root state, the user may just close the browser, which is shown as an arrow leaving the Root state to the statechart's endpoint.

The whole diagram is incredibly simple and yet incredibly powerful when put into use. I realize that may seem like a stretch at this point, but I'm sure that even this simple statechart implemented in code would have a profound effect on the robustness of the application. The reason, this is because we're effectively locking down much of how our application functions. Consider this for example, if we had used an `isSaving` flag we would have to remember to check the value of that flag each time the user clicks on edit, submit or cancel. If we didn't check it or the flag was toggled at the wrong time (race condition), we might accidentally double submit or edit the wrong object. Of course, you would likely disable the respective buttons in the UI based on the `isSaving` flag, but remember that not all actions are always triggered through the user interface. It's simple for someone with malicious intent to open the browser console and try calling improper actions. With our statechart though, we can clearly see that while in the Saving state, none of those actions can occur.

Before we move on, I'd like to introduce a bit more of the statechart theory and expand on what we've seen so far. The first addition is to add history to the default entry point. The concept here is that upon entering a state with substates, we often want to go to the previously entered substate. For example, in a chess game we would have a **Match** state for an active match with two substates **WhitePlays** and **BlackPlays**. When we start a new match, the application would go to the Match state, which would always enter its WhitePlays substate the first time. However, after this point if we left the Match state and re-entered it, we would not want to go directly to WhitePlays, but to whichever substate we were previously in. To do so, we would enter the history state for the Match state, which is represented by a circle with an **H** as shown in the following diagram:

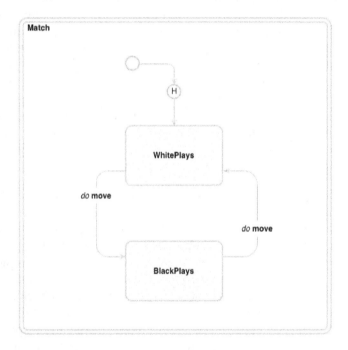

Just as we described, the default entry point is to the history state (one of either WhitePlays or BlackPlays) and as you can tell by the arrow from the H to WhitePlays, if there is no history state, it would go to the WhitePlays state by default.

We can also add more detail to our diagram to reflect how states are entered and exited. Remember that statecharts is a graphical language that will later be translated directly into code; so the more we capture upfront, the less we leave up to interpretation later.

First off, entering and exiting a state will usually perform certain actions, which we can make note of in the diagram. For example, if we were to use a **LogIn** state, we could include actions to present the log in pane and clear the form on entry and to also remove the pane on exit.

Next, event transitions are often dependent on conditions, such as the body of the event or whether the event represents a success or failure. In these cases, the same event type may result in different state transitions according to the event's properties. We can show such conditions in the diagram by including them along with the event name. For instance, every server response may succeed (for example, **HTTP 200 OK**) or may fail (for example, **HTTP 403 Forbidden**) and so a more complete version of the Saving state from the first example could be the following diagram:

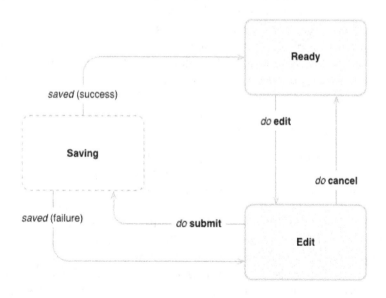

Notice that the **saved** event now contains the success or fail condition in parenthesis. This value indicates the two ways that the saved event will be handled.

While the statecharts language allows for further ways to structure the diagram for readability, we have now captured all of the core features of a statechart with the exception of one, concurrency.

The statecharts language also provides for concurrent states, which allow the statechart to be in multiple states at the same time. On the surface, this doesn't seem overly complex, but it actually adds too many new variables to the discussion to be within the scope of this book. Because concurrent states are more difficult to diagram and to use correctly, I would recommend avoiding them until you have much more experience with the language.

Avoiding pitfalls with statecharts

Remember, to design a statechart is to architect an application, and so creating the statechart diagram should be your first step to programming anything serious. And just like with programming, figuring out the proper statechart is a lot of work and you shouldn't expect to get it right on the first try.

While I can't claim to know every technique to creating a proper statechart diagram, I do know at least a few important rules that we should follow. I have already mentioned that it's better to avoid concurrent states if possible because of the extra complexity and a similar idea is to start simple and grow as needed. Statecharts are particularly well suited for capturing the generalized states for the application quickly and then iteratively adding more specific substates later. Therefore, the first version of your statechart may only include a loading, unauthenticated, and authenticated state and you could actually safely code those states in your app using SproutCore right away. Later, you will likely add several substates to the diagram and likewise, these new states will drop into your code without any refactoring. However, if you start with very granular states right off the bat, you may find yourself having to pull them out again later as the code is written.

A more specific rule-of-thumb is that it's important that states don't change their entry and exit actions dependent on external variables. This just means that, for example, we should not have a Ready state that performs the showLogIn pane action on entry if there is no session, but performs the showMainPane action on entry if there is. To do it like that would mean we've actually got two different states being represented by one. Instead, we should have a **ReadySession** state that will always show the main pane and a **ReadyNoSession** state that will always show the login pane. Then all we need to do is to go to the proper state depending on the session. In this way the ReadySession and ReadyNoSession states can be unit tested, which means more importantly, that they are self-contained.

Keeping states self-contained is the most important rule that I can impart to you. The independence of a state can make the difference between a rock solid application and one that crashes after heavy use. The reason for this is that bugs are often unavoidable. Even the best of us make mistakes and things can, and at some point likely will go wrong. However, if all of our states are independent, when a state has problems, we can usually recover simply by getting out of the state and back into a safe state.

Thinking in terms of state independence will probably be the best tool you will have for defining states. Another easy indication of what constitutes a state is the appending and removal of a pane. If we know we want to show a pane, for example, the main pane, we will definitely have a state that upon entry will show the pane and upon exit will remove the same pane. In this way, the state initializes itself and also cleans itself up, which are two key goals for defining a state. If a state can totally initialize itself and totally clean itself up independent of all the other states, it will be a strong state in your application.

Coding with statecharts

While you can, and should, design statecharts for applications written in any language, only a few frameworks allow you to directly implement the statechart in your code. Fortunately for us, SproutCore is one of those frameworks. What's really amazing is that all the hard work we did designing the statechart diagram takes care of all the logic for our application state layer. All we have to do now is implement the states one-for-one into the code. Let's look at how we do that now.

While you can have multiple statecharts in your application, we only need one to manage the application state. To create a statechart, SproutCore provides the `SC.StatechartManager` mixing that will turn any object into a statechart. While some people like to mix `SC.StatechartManager` into the application object, for example, in `core.js`:

```
MyApp = SC.Application.create(SC.StatechartManager, {
  // ...
});
```

I think it's nice to use a separate statechart `SC.Object`, for example, in a file called `statechart.js`:

```
MyApp.statechart = SC.Object.create(SC.StatechartManager, {
  // ...
});
```

Simply by doing one of the preceding methods, we now have a statechart that we can use to manage our application. The next step is to transcribe what we've diagramed across to the statechart object. Since every statechart has a root state, we would add that state first.

All states in SproutCore are created by extending SC.State and so we simply define the rootState property as follows:

```
MyApp.statechart = SC.Object.create(SC.StatechartManager, {

  rootState: SC.State.extend({
    // ...
  })

});
```

To add substates, simply add them to the appropriate parent state. Remember that any state that has substates should define the initial substate, which is done with the initialSubstate property. Using the first application statechart diagram as an example we would get the following code:

```
MyApp.statechart = SC.Object.create(SC.StatechartManager, {

  rootState: SC.State.extend({
    initialSubstate: 'loadingState',

    loadingState: SC.State,

    readyState: SC.State,

    editState: SC.State,

    savingState: SC.State
  })

});
```

After this we can add the relative state actions and events, which will simply transition to the appropriate state. Building upon the preceding example again, we would have the following code:

```
MyApp.statechart = SC.Object.create(SC.StatechartManager, {

  rootState: SC.State.extend({
    initialSubstate: 'loadingState',
```

```
      loadingState: SC.State.extend({
        didLoad: function () {
          this.gotoState('readyState');
        }
      }),

      readyState: SC.State.extend({
        doEdit: function () {
          this.gotoState('editState');
        }
      }),

      editState: SC.State.extend({
        doCancel: function () {
          this.gotoState('readyState');
        },

        doSubmit: function () {
          this.gotoState('savingState');
        }
      }),

      savingState: SC.State.extend({
        saved: function (successOrFailure) {
          if (successOrFailure) {
            this.gotoState('readyState');
          } else {
            this.gotoState('editState');
          }
        }
      })
    })

  });
```

Wow! Isn't it neat how simply the diagram came across into code and how cleanly we can follow the statechart logic in our code? Do you see how while in a certain state, our application is locked down to the appropriate events and actions for that state? Let's go a little bit further using the other examples.

Another example that we looked at previously used a history state to return to the last substate entered before exiting. Just as we used `gotoState` to move between substates without history, we use `gotoHistoryState` to move between states with history. The following is a Root state we could use for such a chess game:

```
// ...
rootState: SC.State.extend({
  initialSubstate: 'menuState',

  menuState: SC.State.extend({
    // Start a new match.
    startMatch: function () {
      this.gotoState('matchState');
    },

    // Resume the previous match.
    resumeMatch: function () {
      this.gotoHistoryState('matchState');
    }
  }),

  matchState: SC.State.extend({
    initialSubstate: 'whitePlaysState',

    // Pause the match.
    pauseMatch: function () {
      this.gotoState('menuState');
    },

    whitePlaysState: SC.State.extend({
      move: function () {
        this.gotoState('blackPlaysState');
      }
    }),

    blackPlaysState: SC.State.extend({
      move: function () {
        this.gotoState('whitePlaysState');
      }
    })
  })
})
// ...
```

Notice how we simply use `gotoHistoryState` in the `resumeMatch` action when we want to resume our game? It's remarkably easy.

The next item we captured in the example diagrams was our entry and exit actions. The `SC.State` function provides the methods `enterState` and `exitState` to do just this. The next example shows how we would implement the LogIn state from an earlier diagram:

```
logInState: SC.State.extend({

  enterState: function () {
    // Append the log in pane.
    MyApp.logInPage.get('logInPane').append();

    // Reset the form.
    this.resetForm();
  },

  exitState: function () {
    // Remove the log in pane.
    MyApp.logInPage.get('logInPane').remove();
  }

})
```

Finally, we won't want to define all of our states inside of a single file because it will grow too large. Instead, we usually create a `states` directory in the app and give each state its own file. To make this easy, `SC.State` includes a `plugin` method that we use to reference the external state classes. Using our first statechart again as an example, the `statechart.js` file could end up looking something like the following code:

```
MyApp.statechart = SC.Object.create(SC.StatechartManager, {

  rootState: SC.State.extend({
    initialSubstate: 'loadingState',

    loadingState: SC.State.plugin('MyApp.LoadingState'),
    readyState: SC.State.plugin('MyApp.ReadyState'),
    editState: SC.State.plugin('MyApp.EditState'),
    savingState: SC.State.plugin('MyApp.SavingState')
  })

});
```

This makes the statechart file much easier to read now that the code that was previously inside each substate has been moved to its own file. For example, the `MyApp.LoadingState` would be defined in `states/loading_state.js` and would start out with just the subclass definition like the following code:

```
MyApp.LoadingState = SC.State.extend({
  didLoad: function () {
    this.gotoState('readyState');
  }
});
```

There are a few more tricks you can do with SproutCore's statechart library, but that covers everything we want to do so far with statecharts. By the way, to follow along with your new statechart in action, you can set the `trace` property to `true` on the statechart, which will log lots of useful information to the browser's console.

Summary

That wraps up our look at the roles of the Controller and Application State layers in SproutCore. This included a detailed look at SproutCore's controllers and how we use controllers to mediate between our views and models. We also looked at a detailed example of how we can translate raw data from the Model layer into a useful property for the View layer.

We also learned quite a deal about the statecharts language and looked at several applications of statecharts. Most importantly we learned of the important considerations to observe when diagramming the statechart of your own application, including the most important consideration, keeping states self-contained. Lastly we saw how easily we can transcribe the statechart logic into actual code.

Although statecharts is a complex subject for a beginner's tutorial, I've asserted a few times that SproutCore's role is for developing real software, and real software needs real architecture; so I felt that it was important to include. Hopefully this was a bit of an eye-opening experience and you feel more confident than ever in your ability to deliver world-class software with SproutCore.

In the next chapter, we'll wrap up our discussion with a look at testing, building and ultimately deploying a SproutCore application.

6
Testing, Building, and Deploying

At this point we've talked about what SproutCore is, built a simple application, and been into great detail on many of the individual features of the framework, but we haven't yet completed the whole picture. In this chapter we will flesh out some of the remaining pieces so that you're ready to build a real SproutCore application on your own from start to finish.

First, we will look at how to prove out the functionality of your objects and methods using unit tests, which we will see are simple to add to your app. Next, we will look at several options used for configuring the build tools, including proxying requests to avoid same-origin policy restrictions while developing, embedding external JavaScript files and several other common scenarios.

Finally, we will run through the process of building an application in order to deploy it on a web server to make it available to the world. Every deployment is unique, but once we understand exactly what a built SproutCore app is, it will be trivial for you to deploy it on whatever platform you are using.

In this chapter we will cover the following:

- Unit testing SproutCore apps
    - Viewing unit test results
- Using frameworks and modules
- Building and deploying apps
    - Additional configuration options

Unit testing SproutCore apps

I might as well admit it; I am a big fan of unit tests. Once I discovered that unit testing is really a code development tool for improving quality, I've been pretty much sold on them. But first let me explain why I believe unit tests are the best tool for improving the quality of code. Take this simple helper method of a view for example:

```
// Returns the display name of the content
displayName: function (content) {
  if (MyApp.isDownloading  && !this.isReady) {
    return "Downloading…";
  } else {
    return "Name: " + content.name;
  }
}
```

As short as this function is, it still manages to contain a couple of problems that would be highlighted by adding a unit test.

For an instance, it wouldn't take much time to spot problems when writing a unit test that asked "what happens if content is null?" and "what if `content. name` is undefined?". It also wouldn't take long while trying to test this method to discover that the dependency on external variables, `MyApp.isDownloading` and `this.isReady`, makes the method difficult to test. If the component of code can't be isolated and tested as a unit, it is a clear sign of a poorly written component. Obviously, for such a simple method, we can see the problems without needing to test first, but it's easy to miss even simple mistakes when working under stress and deadlines. Plus, we never know who may come in later to tweak a method and unknowingly break an assumption that we had placed in the code. That's why unit tests are also wonderful tools for preventing regressions.

So let's look at unit testing in SproutCore. SproutCore contains the QUnit unit-testing framework that is used by jQuery (`http://qunitjs.com`). If you're familiar with QUnit, you'll already know how to write your unit tests in SproutCore.

Unit tests are contained in the tests directory of an app or framework. If we look at the Contacts app we made in *Chapter 1, Introducing SproutCore*, we will see that by using the command line generators to create our controller and model files, we also got several test stub files as well. Let's revisit the Contacts app and add a few real unit tests.

First let's test the Contact model in `tests/models/contact_test.js`. If you open up the stub file that was generated, it should look something like the following screenshot:

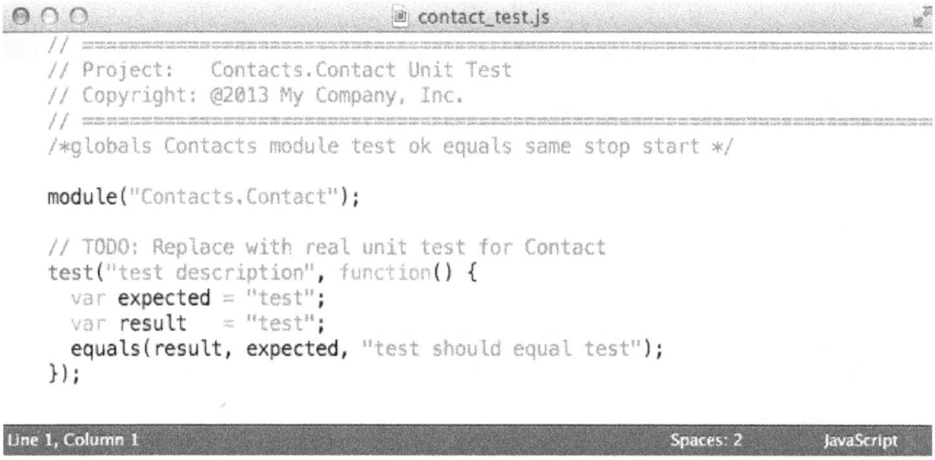

The first function, `module()`, is used for starting a new group of tests. In this case, the group of tests is called `"Contacts.Contact"`. Inside of this module, we see one `test()` function that is passed a description for the test and the function to run. Before we modify this file with actual tests, let's see how we actually run and view the results of the tests.

Viewing unit test results

SproutCore includes an app just for unit testing called **Test Runner** that is available at `http://localhost:4020/sproutcore/tests`. If you simply launch `http://localhost:4020`, you will see it in the list of available apps as `"tests"`. When you do launch the unit-testing app, you will first see all of the apps, frameworks, modules, and themes in the current project listed along with the SproutCore framework that itself includes several apps, sub-frameworks, and themes that can be tested. For example, take a look at the following screenshot:

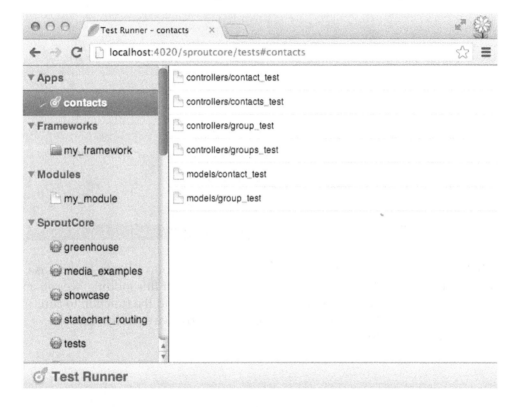

Although you can run the SproutCore unit tests, they are for developers that are working on code within SproutCore to contribute back to the project and so we don't normally care about running them.

Right now, we're only going to focus on tests within the **Apps** section, where we see our **contacts** app is listed. The framework **my_framework** and the module **my_module** are just there for display purposes and don't actually contain any code. I have added them so that I could show how we can test apps, frameworks, and modules all through the single **Test Runner** app. We'll look at creating frameworks and modules later on in this chapter.

To run a suite of tests, we simply select the matching test file from the list. Running our `Contacts.Contact` model test, **models/contact_test**, gives us the following result:

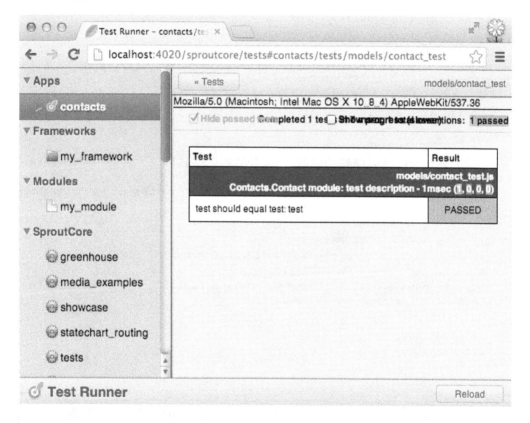

So now it's just a matter of adding as many tests as we can imagine and hitting the **Reload** button to verify the results of the additional tests. Let's try out a couple of QUnits test functions in the `Contacts.Contact` test.

First, we could test the output of the `fullName` computed property to look for problems. Let's do this by replacing the default test with one specific to the `fullName` property, like the following code:

```
test("Test the fullName property: basic tests", function () {
  var store = SC.Store.create(),
    contact;

  // No firstName or lastName.
  contact = store.createRecord(Contacts.Contact, {});
  equals(contact.get('fullName'), '', "`fullName` with no firstName &
lastName should equal");

  // firstName only
  contact = store.createRecord(Contacts.Contact, { firstName: 'Julius'
});
  equals(contact.get('fullName'), 'Julius', "`fullName` with firstName
& no lastName should equal");

  // lastName only
  contact = store.createRecord(Contacts.Contact, { lastName: 'Caesar'
});
  equals(contact.get('fullName'), 'Caesar', "`fullName` with lastName
& no firstName should equal");

  // firstName & lastName
  contact = store.createRecord(Contacts.Contact, { firstName:
'Julius', lastName: 'Caesar' });
  equals(contact.get('fullName'), 'Julius Caesar', "`fullName` with
firstName & lastName should equal");

  // Clean up.
  store.destroy();
});
```

 How you organize your modules and tests is up to you. For debugging purposes, I find it's easier to have a lot of smaller tests with only a few assertions than it is to have large tests with many assertions.

Reloading that test in the browser shows us that all our basic assumptions were correct and all four conditions passed for the test as shown in the following screenshot:

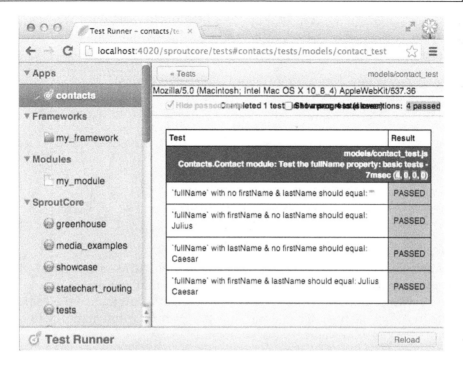

Now for all of our future tests, we will always need to create and destroy a store each time, which would be wasteful. Instead, we can use the setup and teardown options of the module to set up and clean up the common code that all the tests in the module can share.

For example, we could write our `Contacts.Contact` module so that every test has the store object available, shown as follows:

```
var store;
module("Contacts.Contact", {

  setup: function () {
    store = SC.Store.create().from(SC.Record.fixtures);
  },

  teardown: function () {
    store.destroy();
    store = null;
  }

});
```

The final thing you will notice is that I have added the fixtures data source to the store that I have created in the example. When testing models, this makes it really easy to test them thoroughly using the fixture data that you are developing against. As your fixture data grows and becomes more complex, your unit tests can leverage this work to test out more complex scenarios.

For now, here's a simple example showcasing using the fixture data to test a model:

```
test("Test the fullName property: fixtures", function () {
  var contact;

  contact = store.find(Contacts.Contact, 'tyler');
  equals(contact.get('fullName'), 'Tyler Keating', "`fullName` for
'tyler' should equal");
});
```

Now that we've seen how to basically write and run unit tests, we won't dwell on the specifics any further. There are actually over 3,250 unit tests in the SproutCore framework with over 21,300 assertions and so you may want to visit the source on Github to look for examples. That along with the QUnit documentation will help you further improve your unit testing ability.

Using frameworks and modules

One of the challenges of working with large-scale web apps turns out to be just the organization of code. When apps get sufficiently large, it actually becomes a lot of work just finding where things are and knowing where to put new code. We already went over the standard directory structure for an app in *Chapter 1, Introducing SproutCore*, and by sticking to that structure you will have a much easier time organizing the code within your apps. Next though, let's look at ways to split the project into larger components for sharing and optimized delivery.

The first approach is for sharing large components of code between apps by creating frameworks. Frameworks are simply collections of code placed in a folder within the frameworks' directory of the project. In the previous section, you noticed the my_framework framework appeared in the unit tests that was achieved simply by changing into the project directory and typing the following command:

```
$ mkdir frameworks
$ cd frameworks
$ mkdir my_framework
```

Once you have the framework directory, you can work with it much like you would in an app directory. For example, you may want to add a views folder and place some custom views that you've made that you want to share between apps or you may want to add a resources folder and add a shared log in pane that multiple apps will use. In this way, you can pull the larger architectural pieces out of the app code and into a framework so that you don't end up duplicating the code across every app.

To include the framework in the app, you add it to the list of required frameworks in the **Buildfile**. For example, to include a framework of custom view components called `my_views` to the contacts app, we would modify the Buildfile in `apps/contacts` shown as follows:

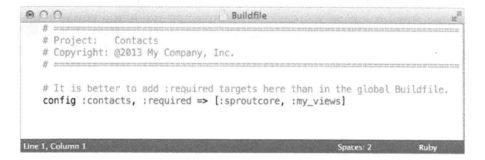

```ruby
#
# Project:   Contacts
# Copyright: @2013 My Company, Inc.
#

# It is better to add :required targets here than in the global Buildfile.
config :contacts, :required => [:sproutcore, :my_views]
```

In this example, when the application is built the `sproutcore` framework will be included first, followed by the `my_views` framework, and then the `contacts` app code. Since frameworks can also include their own Buildfiles, you could actually ensure that the correct order is always followed by adding a Buildfile to the framework.

For example, we can ensure that the `my_views` framework always has the `sproutcore` framework that it depends on shown as follows:

```ruby
#
# Project:   MyViews Framework
# Copyright: @2013 My Company, Inc.
#

# It is better to add :required targets here than in the global Buildfile.
config :my_views, :required => [:sproutcore]
```

By setting the requirement for the supporting framework, we are safe if someone were to use that framework later and fail to require `sproutcore` first.

By the way, a possible optimization that you can make for your app load time is to exclude any SproutCore frameworks that you are not using. By default, requiring `sproutcore` in the Buildfile is the same as requiring the following code:

```
config :my_app, :required => [
  :'sproutcore/desktop',
  :'sproutcore/datastore',
  :'sproutcore/statechart'
]
```

Typically, you will end up using almost all the code available in these sub-frameworks, but if you were writing a very simple app and found you weren't using one or more of them, you can exclude it to reduce the amount of code to deliver to the client. For example, you could exclude the desktop framework with the following code:

```
config :my_app, :required => [
  :'sproutcore/datastore',
  :'sproutcore/statechart'
]
```

Again though, this removes several important SproutCore views that you probably won't be able to function without in any decently sized application. A better option then is to load code through modules.

Modules are very similar to frameworks, they are just bundles of code that provide a specific purpose, but they have one distinct advantage over frameworks and that is modules can be deferred until they are actually needed.

Take the Contacts app for example. Imagine if we had a complex account administration pane for the user's account, but that we expected them to rarely open it. In that case, we wouldn't benefit by including the code and styling for the account pane along with the regular app, since there was little chance that it would be used. Instead, we would be better off loading it but not passing it until later or not even loading it at all unless the user wants to open the pane.

This is what modules provide us. We can package a section of the app into a module and either load it as a string in the initial app code, as a string in a separate file slightly after launching, or not load it at all until required.

To create a module, simply add a `modules` directory to an app or a framework. Within that modules directory, you can then add multiple modules just like you would add frameworks. For example, to add an `account_mgmt` module to the `MyApp` app, I would change to the app directory and type the following command:

```
$ cd apps/my_app
$ mkdir modules
$ cd modules
$ mkdir modules/account_mgmt
```

Within the `account_mgmt` module, we can add views, resources, and even stylesheets that will be loaded on demand when needed.

Once we've created the module, we simply need to indicate how to load it via the app's Buildfile. For example, here is a sample app with three different load styles of modules:

```ruby
#
# -------------------------------------------------------------------
# Project:   MyApp
# Copyright: @2013 My Company, Inc.
# -------------------------------------------------------------------
#

# It is better to add :required targets here than in the global Buildfile.
config :my_app, :required => :sproutcore,

  # Inlines and defers parsing of these modules until they are requested.
  :inlined_modules => [
    :'my_app/preferences'
  ],

  # Fetches but defers parsing of these modules until they are requested.
  :prefetched_modules => [
    :'my_app/log_in'
  ],

  # Defers loading and parsing of these modules until they are requested.
  :deferred_modules => [
    :'my_app/account_mgmt'
  ]
```

Line 1, Column 1   Spaces: 2   Ruby

The following is a more complete description of each module option:

- **Inlined**: These modules are embedded as strings into the app code, so there isn't a separate file request required. An inlined module will always be available in the app, which makes them suitable for offline apps.

- **Prefetched**: These modules are embedded as strings in separate files that will be loaded after the application has launched and user activity is idle for one second. This makes prefetched modules better for improving initial load times than inlined modules, but a prefetched requires running the app online for a bit before being able to safely go offline.

- **Deferred**: These modules are not loaded at all in the app unless requested. This makes deferred modules the best for improving initial load times and runtime memory usage, but they cannot be used for code required in offline mode. They also have a longer initial use delay, since the code needs to be downloaded right before being used.

Once you have determined how you want your modules included, you can use them in your app very easily. To load a module, simply call SC.Module.loadModule with the name of the module and a target and method to call when it is loaded. Best of all, if the module is already loaded, you can still call SC.Module.loadModule at any time and the target/method will simply run immediately, so you don't need to check if a module is loaded yet or not.

For example, to load the log_in module from the preceding example, we would use the following code:

```
SC.Module.loadModule('my_app/log_in', targetObject,
    targetObject.logInModuleDidLoad);
```

The targetObject.logInModuleDidLoad() function would then proceed to use the code included in the module. As you can probably guess, this works exceptionally well with the application statechart. We can create a state around a module's code and call loadModule whenever we enter the state.

Building and deploying apps

Now that we've gone through every step from creating an app to testing it, we're ready to actually deploy our work. This is quite easily done with SproutCore's build tools, you just need to have an understanding of what a built and deployed SproutCore app really is. Remember, SproutCore apps are just static files that run in the client. There is no need for a special app server, any web server will do.

First off, when we work on the app in "debug" mode (that is, locally), we have code and styles split across several files that are served individually to the browser using a development server, sproutcore server. But when we are ready to deploy the app, we want to build it in "production" mode so that it can be properly served remotely to the end user.

There are two important objectives of a production ready web app, the first is that it should load extremely fast and the second is that it should be correctly cacheable. To achieve the first objective, when SproutCore builds our app, the multiple files are concatenated into a single JavaScript file and a single stylesheet file that are then minified to remove whitespace and comments and to greatly compact the code. While a working project may be a few megabytes of code, comments, and whitespace; the minified version will be a fraction of that. Also, because the code is compiled into a single file, it requires only one request from the user's browser that is significantly faster than multiple requests each with added latency. When you add `gzip` compression to the files, you will find that even gigantic SproutCore apps load faster than the typical blog or news site.

Concatenation of the files is done alphabetically unless there is an `sc_require` directive found in the file. The `sc_require` directive informs the build tools that a separate file is required first and should take the form of `sc_require('path_from_app_root_to_other_file')`.

For example, in `my_app/resources/main_page.js`, we would require the file `my_app/views/my_view.js` using the following:

```
sc_require('views/my_view');
```

To achieve the second objective, to be cached correctly, SproutCore outputs our app to a unique path. Properly caching and invalidating cached resources is a very tricky process. If we use a fixed path to our resources each time we deploy a new version, it would not appear to the end user until they cleared their browser cache. Obviously, we want all our users to be using the latest version that may be the only version that works with the current API for instance. On the other hand, if we use a process like appending random numbers to the end of the resource URLs when we request them, we will be preventing the files from being cached and the user would be re-downloading the code on each reload. What SproutCore does is that it generates a hash path for each unique build that ensures that the resource is cacheable and that new builds properly invalidate the cache. We'll look at how to deploy a SproutCore app considering the hash path in a moment, but first let's build an app.

Using our Contacts app for example, we simply change to the project and type the following command:

```
$ sproutcore build contacts
```

Where `sproutcore build` (`sc-build` for short) is the command and `contacts` is the name of the app we want to build. Have a look at the following screenshot:

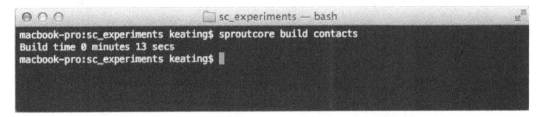

This creates a new directory in the project's `tmp` directory called `build`, in which we will find the built version of the app inside of a directory called `static`.

This `static` directory is the directory that you're going to want to upload to a web server somewhere to make your app public. So it really is just about as easy as running the build command and copying the static directory over to your web server, except for one thing. If you inspect the static directory, you will find that the path to the generated `index.html` file is something similar to the following:

static/contacts/en/18fd57681cc926bbc3c49d6d58f7ae41f95cebe2/index.html

> The actual path will differ on your system, because the hash portion (for example, `18fd57681cc926bbc3c49d6d58f7ae41f95cebe2`) is unique and changes for each new build of the application. Having unique hashes is of critical importance, as it ensures that assets are cached properly so that users aren't re-downloading assets unnecessarily or using stale assets.

Now you obviously wouldn't want your users to type a URL like `http://{my_app_domain}/static/contacts/en/{some_long_hash}` each time to launch your app. So there is a third step to take after copying the files to your web server, that is, to either move the `index.html` file to the root of the web server directory alongside the static directory or to symbolically link to the `index.html` file inside of `static` from within the root of the web server.

Moving the `index.html` file is actually not recommended because when you redeploy, you will end up overwriting the previous `index.html` file that could make it impossible to rollback your deployment. Instead, it's better to keep several builds deployed on the server and simply switch the symbolic link to the most recent version. That way if there are any problems, you can quickly rollback your deployment to a previous version by simply changing the link.

For example, on the server you would perform something like the following command after copying the new build over:

```
$ cd /var/www
$ ln -is static/contacts/en/{NEW_BUILD_NUMBER}/index.html index.html
```

And there you have it, a live SproutCore application is deployed in only a few steps that you can easily automate in the future if you like.

Additional configuration options

Before we finish up, let's take one final moment to go through a few more Buildfile configuration options that you can use for more complex requirements. The first option you will definitely use is the :title option. This simply sets the value of the <title> element in the <head>. For example, have a look at the following code:

```
config :my_app,
  :title => "My Wonderful App"
```

Another option you will likely use at some point is :javascript_libs. This option allows you to specify external JavaScript files to include in your application. For example, to include the Google Maps API in an app, we would add the following code to the Buildfile:

```
config :my_app,
  :javascript_libs => [
    'https://maps.googleapis.com/maps/api/js?v=3&sensor=false'
  ]
```

Likewise we can include external stylesheets using the :stylesheet_libs configuration option.

Another option useful for deploying SproutCore apps in a native wrapper is the :build_number option. This will actually always build the app to a fixed path so that it is easier to include as static files inside of another project. For example, have a look at the following code:

```
config :my_app,
  :build_number => 'latest'
```

Be warned though, fixed paths should never be used for an app served from a web server, since caching will not work correctly.

Lastly, you can also specify configurations depending on the build mode that allows you to more easily keep the debug, testing, and production code separate. For example, if I were to use analytics in an app, I would not want it to log while developing or testing the app. One approach I might take is to put the analytics code in a framework that I would only require in production mode like the following code:

```
mode :production do
  config :my_app,
    required => ['analytics']
end
```

If I wanted to ensure that my code ran unaffected in debug mode, I might create a dummy analytics framework with placeholder functions that do nothing and include it like the following code:

```
mode :debug do
  config :my_app,
    required => ['dummy_analytics']
end
```

> The default mode of `sproutcore server` is `debug` and the default mode of `sproutcore build` is `production`, but you can easily change that by passing `--mode=mode` to the command.

There are a few other options for manipulating the build that you can learn about in the SproutCore Guides at `http://guides.sproutcore.com`, but these few options are likely the only ones you'll ever need.

Summary

And, with that we complete our walkthrough of SproutCore. I hope that you found it both informative and invigorating and that you now feel ready to tackle ambitious new web apps. There is a lot in SproutCore that means you will likely want to keep this book around for your future reference from time-to-time, but more importantly it means that there is a lot of potential in SproutCore for you to tap into and develop genre defining web apps. Once you get really good at leveraging the work that went into SproutCore, you will find that you are able to create powerful web apps in incredibly short times.

While there are a few small areas that we have left for a more advanced discussion, you now have all the information you need to build a production quality application from start to finish. As you do, be sure to visit the SproutCore mailing list at `sproutcore@googlegroups.com` and the community channel `#sproutcore` on IRC to get support from myself and many others in the community.

Index

Thank you for buying
SproutCore Web Application Development

About Packt Publishing

Packt, pronounced 'packed', published its first book "*Mastering phpMyAdmin for Effective MySQL Management*" in April 2004 and subsequently continued to specialize in publishing highly focused books on specific technologies and solutions.

Our books and publications share the experiences of your fellow IT professionals in adapting and customizing today's systems, applications, and frameworks. Our solution based books give you the knowledge and power to customize the software and technologies you're using to get the job done. Packt books are more specific and less general than the IT books you have seen in the past. Our unique business model allows us to bring you more focused information, giving you more of what you need to know, and less of what you don't.

Packt is a modern, yet unique publishing company, which focuses on producing quality, cutting-edge books for communities of developers, administrators, and newbies alike. For more information, please visit our website: www.packtpub.com.

About Packt Open Source

In 2010, Packt launched two new brands, Packt Open Source and Packt Enterprise, in order to continue its focus on specialization. This book is part of the Packt Open Source brand, home to books published on software built around Open Source licences, and offering information to anybody from advanced developers to budding web designers. The Open Source brand also runs Packt's Open Source Royalty Scheme, by which Packt gives a royalty to each Open Source project about whose software a book is sold.

Writing for Packt

We welcome all inquiries from people who are interested in authoring. Book proposals should be sent to author@packtpub.com. If your book idea is still at an early stage and you would like to discuss it first before writing a formal book proposal, contact us; one of our commissioning editors will get in touch with you.

We're not just looking for published authors; if you have strong technical skills but no writing experience, our experienced editors can help you develop a writing career, or simply get some additional reward for your expertise.

Sencha Touch Mobile
JavaScript Framework

Build web applications for Apple iOS and Google Android
touchscreen devices with this first HTML5 mobile framework

John E. Clark
Bryan P. Johnson

PACKT open source ✽

Sencha Touch Mobile JavaScript Framework

ISBN: 978-1-849515-10-8 Paperback: 316 pages

Build web applications for Apple iOS and Google
Android touchscreen devices with this first HTML5
mobile framework

1. Learn to develop web applications that look
   and feel native on Apple iOS and Google
   Android touchscreen devices using Sencha
   Touch through examples

2. Design resolution-independent and graphical
   representations like buttons, icons, and tabs of
   unparalleled flexibility

3. Add custom events like tap, double tap, swipe,
   tap and hold, pinch, and rotate

Django JavaScript Integration:
AJAX and jQuery

Develop AJAX applications using Django and jQuery

Jonathan Hayward

PACKT open source ✽

Django JavaScript Integration: AJAX and jQuery

ISBN: 978-1-849510-34-9 Paperback: 324 pages

Develop AJAX applications using Django and jQuery

1. Learn how Django + jQuery = AJAX

2. Integrate your AJAX application with Django
   on the server side and jQuery on the client side

3. Learn how to handle AJAX requests with jQuery

4. Compare the pros and cons of client-side search
   with JavaScript and initializing a search on the
   server side via AJAX

Please check **www.PacktPub.com** for information on our titles

Joomla! 1.5 JavaScript jQuery

ISBN: 978-1-849512-04-6   Paperback: 292 pages

Enhance your Joomla! sites with the power of jQuery extensions, plugins, and more

1. Build impressive Joomla! Sites with JavaScript and jQuery

2. Create your own Joomla!, jQuery-powered, extensions

3. Enhance your site with third-party features, code-highlighting, Flicker, and more using Joomla! Plugins

4. Detailed explanations with step-by-step guidance and practical examples

Dreamweaver CS6 Mobile and Web Development with HTML5, CSS3, and jQuery Mobile

ISBN: 978-1-849694-74-2   Paperback: 268 pages

Harness the cutting-edge features of Dreamweaver for mobile and web development

1. A basic, compressed, updated introduction to building advanced web sites with Dreamweaver

2. A focused exploration of employing cutting edge HTML5 techniques such as native media

3. An in-depth explanation of how to build inviting, accessible mobile sites with Dreamweaver CS6, responsive design, and jQuery Mobile

Please check **www.PacktPub.com** for information on our titles

www.ingramcontent.com/pod-product-compliance
Lightning Source LLC
Chambersburg PA
CBHW080412060326
40689CB00019B/4219